W9-AWA-799

Sounds Good

Over 100 favourite recipes shared by Festival Musicians

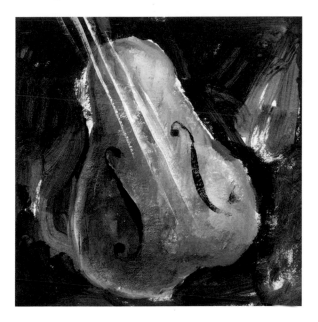

Festival of the Sound
Parry Sound

Copyright © 2006 by Festival of the Sound

All rights reserved.

No portion of this book may be reproduced—mechanically, electronically, or by any other means, including photocopying—without the written permission of the publisher.

LIBRARY AND ARCHIVES CANADA CATALOGUING IN PUBLICATION

   Sounds good : over 100 favourite recipes shared by Festival musicians.

Includes index.
ISBN 0-9781196-0-6

   1. Cookery.   I. Festival of the Sound (Parry Sound, Ont.)

TX714.S649 2006   641.5   C2006-903076-6

Published by Festival of the Sound
Box 750, Parry Sound, Ontario P2A 2Z1
info@festivalofthesound.ca   www.festivalofthesound.ca

Book design and illustrations: Sara Tyson

10 9 8 7 6 5 4 3 2 1

Printed in Canada.

All product/brand names are trademarks or registered trademarks of their respective trademark holders.

Disclaimer: We have taken care to ensure that the information in this book is accurate. However, we can give no absolute guarantees as to the accuracy or completeness of the content of this book. We accept no liability for any losses or damages (whether direct, indirect, special, consequential, or otherwise) arising out of errors or omissions contained in this book.

Callawind
Custom Cookbooks

Produced by Callawind Custom Cookbooks
A division of Callawind Publications Inc.
3551 St. Charles Boulevard, Suite 179, Kirkland, Quebec H9H 3C4
E-mail: info@callawind.com   Website: www.callawind.com
Copy editing: Shaun Oakey   Indexing: Heather Ebbs

Dedication

To the Festival Presidents:
those visionary individuals who have given a year or more of their lives
to lead, inspire, provoke, and push Festival Board members,
staff, and musicians toward excellence.

Eileen Jennings
Cameron Murch
Betty Kyl-Heku
Peter Maule
Maurice Wilkinson
Doris Brown
Glenna Powell
Bob Lederman
Alan Stein
Anne Marie Hoelscher
Janis Ryder
Mary Sallinen
John Sallinen
Elizabeth Browne
Patricia Mueller
Gordon Rempel
Margaret Ibey

Contents

ANDRÉ BENETEAU

Acknowledgements

The Festival of the Sound thanks all of the musicians, Board members, staff, and Festival friends who have contributed to *Sounds Good*. All proceeds from the sale of this book will support the future seasons of the Festival of the Sound.

The Festival of the Sound gratefully acknowledges the support of the Heaman Family Foundation, which made the publication of *Sounds Good* possible.

Margie Boyd and Heather Krause each gained ten pounds while editing, proofing, and rewriting such interesting recipes, not from sampling the food but from the chocolate-covered jujubes readily available at Kitchen Cupboard Bulk Foods right next door to the Festival Office.

Sara Tyson is responsible for the design of *Sounds Good* and generously contributed the illustrations for the cover and inside pages. Marcy Claman of Callawind Custom Cookbooks handled the production of the book and kept us all on schedule.

Special thanks are due to two Past Presidents:
Glenna Powell, who spearheaded the 10th Anniversary cookbook, *Sounds Good,* in 1989 and who summed up the Festival of the Sound so beautifully in her "Recipe for a Great Festival" (see page 11). Glenna brought along a copy of this recipe in what would be her last visit to the Festival Office in the summer of 2005. Her untimely death in November of 2005 is a great loss to the Festival family. Elizabeth Browne, who spearheaded this cookbook project and worked tirelessly to bring it to publication. There were many points along the way at which everyone else became discouraged and ready to abandon the idea. But Liz never gave up, and, under her leadership, this beautiful book is now a reality.

Testers:
For the two years leading up to the publication of *Sounds Good,* Parry Sound kitchens were full of wonderful smells and Festival potlucks were even more bountiful than usual, as all the recipes from musicians were tested and enjoyed. Thank you to all of the testers listed here, and to the tasters among their families and friends. Special acknowledgements are due to Leslie Crawford, who reviewed every recipe with the eye of a gourmet cook.

Marg Allan	Ruth Gray	Katy McNabb	Shirley Stott
Maxine Begy	Roy Hardie	Laura McNabb	Maureen Thompson
Margie Boyd	Anne Marie Hoelscher	Margaret McNabb	Daniel Verité
Liz Browne	Margaret Ibey	Marlene Mooy	Mara Vielands
Bob and Bev Burnham	Ruth and Don Inkpen	Josephine Oxley	Arlene Weimer
Hazel Carpenter	Yani Kelly	Gladys Pountney	Bridget Wells
Leslie Crawford	Nancy Little	Sharon Ranney	Judith White
Gini Donker	Alice McIntyre	Jan and Gordon Rempel	
Barbara Fisher	Joanne McLean	Jane Ross	
Marge Flynn	Bev McNabb	Alan Stein	

ANDRÉ BENETEAU

Introduction

The 1980 Festival of the Sound marked the beginning of Ontario's first annual international summer festival of classical music. During the summer of 1979, renowned pianist Anton Kuerti purchased a summer home near Parry Sound and organized three concerts by outstanding Canadian musicians. The enthusiastic response to these programs inspired him to propose an annual concert series. A number of local residents accepted the challenge, and the Festival of the Sound was born with Mr. Kuerti as Artistic Director.

In 1985, James Campbell began his tenure as the Festival's second Artistic Director, a position that he still holds today with distinction. The volunteer Board of Directors works all year with Margie Boyd, the Executive Director, and Jim to prepare for the summer concert series, which has grown from a two-week festival with an annual budget of $60,000 in 1980 to a three-week festival with a $675,000 budget in 2006. The Festival of the Sound was honoured in 1995 and again in 2003 with a Lieutenant Governor's Award for the Arts in recognition of the exceptional private sector and community support developed over the years.

Hundreds of Canadian and international musicians have performed at the Festival during its 27 years. Among musicians and music-lovers alike, the Festival of the Sound has an outstanding reputation for the excellence of its programming and for the warm and welcoming environment in which it is presented. A loyal group of friends and supporters was built during 23 seasons when the main performance venue was the small gym in Parry Sound High School. The seats were hard, the sightlines were poor, and the heat was often unbearable. But the joy experienced as great music was shared was infectious.

Perhaps because it took 23 years to achieve a beautiful setting in which to enjoy the performances, the sharing of great food, beautifully presented, took on great significance in the life of the Festival family. Flutist Suzanne Shulman shares her memories of those years: "Right now my thoughts about food and the Festival go back to all those years in the teachers' lounge at the Parry Sound High School. Performers would be waiting for their turn to play, draped over chairs in the heat, with their assorted children sometimes listening to the music or watching the baseball game on TV! There was lots of laughter at the jokes (usually Jim Mason's!), the ladies trying to claim the washroom as their own, and the whole time the wonderful volunteers would be in and out of the kitchen, making sure that there was enough water and lemonade to keep everyone hydrated. Then at the end as everyone returned to the lounge from the stage there would be a delicious spread of fresh fruits and cheese and pastries for the hungry musicians, CBC crew, friends and family. After the heat of the gym, those refreshments were so welcome (and still are

JULIAN STEIN

in the new Stockey Centre!). So here's a salute to those dedicated volunteers who work so hard to keep us a happy company!"

Volunteers who were involved in the start-up years recall baking and selling cookies to raise money for the postage to send out the first season brochures. For the first Gala Opening concert in 1980, hors d'oeuvres prepared by Board members were served. Since the budget seldom allowed for

catered events, many volunteers discovered talents they didn't know they had. A review of the photo albums shows a rabbi cooking at a barbecue, a United Church minister and a retired engineer, both over six feet tall, bent over the sinks washing dishes, a physician setting out plates at a Sunday brunch, and realtors serving coffee and muffins before an early-morning island concert. Many residents of the Parry Sound area have graciously shared their beautiful homes for concerts, always of course accompanied by wonderful food. Gallons of iced tea and lemonade refreshed concertgoers who poured from the hot gymnasium at intermission. Few could resist the Dilly Bars sold by members of the Festival's Junior Guild.

At the 2003 opening of the spectacular Charles W. Stockey Centre for the Performing Arts, on the Parry Sound waterfront, James Campbell walked on stage to say, "Well, dreams do come true." The Charles W. Stockey Festival Performance Hall has quickly gained a reputation as one of the world's finest for performing and listening to chamber music. The seats are comfortable, the sightlines are excellent, and the air conditioning is efficient and silent. The beautiful granite walls and the exposed wood in the high peaked ceiling give it the warmth and charm of a Georgian Bay cottage. Audience members gather on the bayside deck at intermission to drink in the sunsets over the Big Sound. And young volunteers still pass through the crowds, offering nuts, truffles, and other irresistible delicacies.

As part of its 10th anniversary celebrations in 1989, the Festival of the Sound produced its first edition of *Sounds Good,* under the direction of President Glenna Powell. Glenna wrote the recipe on the next page to introduce that book.

Liz Browne served as Festival President in 2001 and 2002, the challenging years during which the new concert hall was built. Resources were stretched to the maximum as Board members, past Presidents, and staff served key roles on the Building, Fundraising, and Operations Committees as well as doing the work to keep the Festival growing and successful. In addition to making financial contributions to the building project, the Festival Board had to double its operating budget to meet the new challenges and opportunities that would come its way. In suggesting the production of a book of recipes by Festival musicians, Liz helped to keep everyone grounded, embracing the exciting challenges that came our way without losing sight of the vision and goals of our founders, as so beautifully expressed in "A Recipe for a Great Festival." We hope that you will enjoy *Sounds Good* and thank you for supporting the Festival of the Sound through its purchase.

ANDRÉ BENETEAU

Recipe for a Great Festival

1 dream of celebrating great music and the beauty of Parry Sound

1 moderate-sized group of classical music lovers

2 very different, creative Artistic Directors, Anton Kuerti and James Campbell

10 Boards of Directors

Countless volunteers

10 small groups of staff

Attentive audiences

Generous donors

Gifted artists

Outstanding chamber music

The best of jazz for spice

Georgian Bay sunsets

Musical Cruises aboard the *Island Queen*

Great acoustics of the Parry Sound High School auditorium

Nature Walks

Brunches

Children's Concerts

Love

Delicious food

Stir together gently so that no component is bruised or diminished.
Allow to grow carefully for 49 weeks each year.
Serve splendidly with excitement and fanfare for three weeks each July and August.

VARIATION:
Add 1 dream of a physically comfortable and aesthetically and acoustically pleasing
Concert Hall on the shores of Georgian Bay.

— *Glenna Powell, 1989*

FROM TOP: (1) ALAN STEIN; (3) BEV MCNABB; (4,5) JULIAN STEIN

Special Guests

The Inn at Manitou
Little Britt Inn
Log Cabin Inn
Resort Tapatoo
The Ridge at Manitou

The Inn at Manitou
Manitouwabing Lake
McKellar, Ontario
www.manitou-online.com
1-800-571-8818

The Inn at Manitou

The Inn at Manitou is open Spring, Summer and Fall with changing menus to characterize the seasons. Nestled on the shores of Manitouwabing Lake, one of Ontario's most beautiful unspoiled lakes, 150 miles north of Toronto, the Inn is a small luxury resort hotel of only 35 rooms. Surrounded by forests and rocky shoreline, we are a member of the distinguished Paris based Relais et Châteaux Association.

Rooms at the Inn are all charming, handsomely appointed and range in size and opulence from standard to large and grandly furnished. Our kitchen uses only best quality fresh products whatever the cost, to ensure guest satisfaction and maintain the Inn's enviable reputation for culinary excellence. We are proud to offer our guests a personal fitness, health and beauty Spa program and have never forgotten our roots as a tennis resort. Our efforts in creating the Inn and offering our superb cuisine, sports programs and spa are a labour of love and source of great satisfaction.

Venison Tenderloin with Blueberries and Spicy Pepper Sauce

BERNARD IBANEZ
Head Chef, The Inn at Manitou

Chef Bernard is returning for a sixth summer to The Inn at Manitou after spending the winter in China, always looking for new ingredients and new dishes to tempt our guests.

Bernard Ibanez is French, having trained at D'Ecole Hotelier Paris and has worked as Head Chef in many countries including Mexico, France and Asia.

1 Clean the tenderloin and set aside the trimmings for the sauce. Cut into 8 sections, roll in coarse ground black pepper and set in cool place.

2 Add olive oil to a sauté pan to brown the venison, add the leek, carrot, onion, garlic and sweat.

3 Deglaze with Sherry vinegar and reduce until dry. Deglaze with red wine, reduce and add pepper, clove, bay leaf, orange zest, thyme, veal stock and blueberries. Boil and skim. Cover and simmer on low heat for 30 to 40 minutes.

4 Pour the liquid through a Chinese strainer. Reduce and set aside. Taste, and season with salt and pepper. Reheat just before serving.

5 Season the tenderloin and sauté in a non-stick frying pan to the desired temperature.

6 Place wilted spinach in the centre of the plate and put the tenderloin on the spinach. Pour sauce over the tenderloin. Serve with sweet potato chips.

Enjoy your meal!

YIELD: 4 servings

Copyright 2005 Bernard Ibanez, The Inn at Manitou

700 grams venison tenderloin

1 tablespoon butter

2 tablespoons coarse ground black pepper

VENISON SAUCE

500 grams venison trimmings in cubes

1 white leek, chopped

1 carrot, peeled and chopped

1 onion, peeled and chopped

2 cloves garlic, peeled and crushed

30 centilitres red wine

20 grams coarse ground black pepper

1 clove

1 sprig thyme

1 bay leaf

200 grams blueberries

1 tablespoon orange zest

50 centilitres veal stock

4 centilitres Sherry vinegar

3 tablespoons olive oil

Little Britt Inn
Byng Inlet
Britt, Ontario
google us
1-888-383-4555

Little Britt Inn

Located on Georgian Bay north of Parry Sound in the community of Britt, the Little Britt Inn is a small world class Inn. Jim Sorrenti and Teri McLean have, over the past 14 years, transformed the Inn into four overnight suites and two restaurants.

The atmosphere is relaxed and casual in both restaurants. The upper deck restaurant is a large screened deck area overlooking the water. It takes local fare to a higher level with the rack of Manitoulin lamb, bacon wrapped elk medallions, oysters on the half shell and Georgian Bay chowder. An extensive collection of wine is kept on display.

The lower deck, which also doubles as an oyster bar in the busy season, offers an excellent menu with house favourites such as yellow perch, pickerel and beef tenderloin, Teri's ever changing soups (billed as Yesterday's Soups) and their world famous bread pudding. In the off-season you can arrange small intimate dinners for four couples, complete with overnight accommodations and breakfast.

Pickerel Poached in Tomato Consommé

TERI McLEAN
Head of Kitchen, Little Britt Inn

Except for a short period, working with the head chef at Westover Inn and a winter at Stratford chef school, Teri is self-taught. She is continually experimenting and developing her own style. A good example is the feature recipe. Having mastered the tomato consommé to her liking and wanting to try poaching pickerel for her diet conscious customers, a new dish at The Little Britt Inn was born.

This type of creativity is responsible for the Little Britt Inn being listed in "Where To Eat In Canada" for the past six years.

1 Drizzle the plum tomatoes with olive oil and roast for 40 minutes in a 375°F oven.

2 Chop the onion, garlic, leek, carrot, and fennel, saving the fennel fronds for garnish.

3 Cook until tender in large well oiled pot.

4 Add the chicken stock and the roasted tomatoes. Bring to a boil and let simmer for 20 minutes.

5 Pass mixture through a food mill. Reheat resulting liquid to a boil, add saffron, salt and pepper to taste, reduce to simmer and add ouzo.

6 Poach the pickerel fillets in consommé.

7 Carefully transfer the fillets to heated soup plates and pour the consommé over them.

8 Finally, garnish with fennel fronds.

— *Teri McLean*

12 plum tomatoes, halved

2 tablespoons olive oil

1 large onion

4 cloves garlic

1 stalk leek

1 large carrot

1 head fennel

4 cups chicken stock

¼ teaspoon saffron

Salt

Pepper

1 ounce ouzo

8 pickerel fillets, approximately 1 to 1½ pounds each

Log Cabin Inn
Oastler Park Drive
Parry Sound, Ontario
www.logcabininn.net
705-746-7122

Log Cabin Inn

The Log Cabin Inn is Parry Sound's best-kept secret. This small intimate country Inn north of Toronto provides the perfect ambience for its fine dining and extensive wine list.

This four-season Inn is the perfect choice for taking a quiet getaway or enjoying a wide range of year round activities. Located in a beautiful country setting, our individual luxury chalets are spacious, tastefully decorated and are each equipped with Jacuzzi, fireplace and many other amenities. We feature great year round getaway packages!

The Inn includes a newly enlarged dining room and high speed Internet. We also offer off site catering for weddings, business meetings and all occasion parties.

Kathy and Paul Crepeau are owner operators who take pride in their gem! You will find Paul and Kathy's personal touches in all aspects of the business. Whether greeting guests or planting their gardens, these owners are hands on and quite accessible.

Come let us spoil you.

Duck Confit

DAVID CHIASSON
Chef, Log Cabin Inn

Dave hails from Newmarket, Ontario. He attended George Brown College in Toronto for Culinary Arts. After working in Southern Ontario he followed his love of the Muskokas and headed North.

Dave finds he receives a natural high from channeling his creativity into the preparation of delicious food! He is an integral part of a team at Log Cabin Inn and has been instrumental in the planning of many successful events such as the West Parry Sound Health Centre Galas. Dave excels at sharing his love of his craft with young apprentices. Dave enjoys working with the best quality products and finding freedom of expression in mastering his culinary art.

1. Combine bay leaves, juniper berries and peppercorns. Toast lightly and crush. Mix the crushed spices with sea salt and sugar. Rough chop the parsley, thyme, garlic and shallots. Add these ingredients to the cure.

2. Put the duck legs skin side down on a wire rack. Completely cover with the cure. Cover and refrigerate for 5 hours.

3. Remove duck from refrigerator and wash the cure off the duck with fresh water. Dry the duck legs.

4. Place the duck legs in a frying pan on low heat. Render until skin becomes crispy. Remove from heat and place duck legs in a roasting pan. Completely cover the duck legs with duck fat. Place in oven and cook at 200°F for 8 hours.

5. Remove legs from the fat. Return the meat to the hot oven and roast until crispy.

YIELD: 4 servings

— *David Chiasson*

12 bay leaves

20 juniper berries

20 black peppercorns

8 tablespoons coarse sea salt

8 tablespoons sugar

½ bunch Italian parsley

10 sprigs thyme

5 cloves garlic

5 shallots

8 large duck legs

4 litres duck fat

Resort Tapatoo
Otter Lake
Parry Sound, Ontario
www.tapatoo.com
1-800-461-5410

Resort Tapatoo

Resort Tapatoo, located on a quiet wooded peninsula surrounded by the brilliant waters of Otter Lake, takes great pride in offering the finest in personal service and attention.

It is a full service year round deluxe resort with your hosts Guenter and Christa Siebert, owners and operators, catering to all types of clientele. Tapatoo opened with 10 cottages and the Black Forest House in 1986 and has grown to a charming 61-room resort and conference facility. Guests may enjoy our heated indoor pool, refreshing sauna, whirlpool hot tub, fitness room and spa.

The Blackforest House, home to our front desk, restaurant, dining rooms and lounge, retains the intimate charm of its German origins. The exceptional cuisine of Chef Roy Hintze is offered daily in dining rooms famous for their spectacular views of Otter Lake. Resort Tapatoo offers a quiet secluded waterfront disturbed only by the call of the loon.

Labour Day Mushroom Chowder

ROY HINTZE, C.C.C.
Chef, Resort Tapatoo

The gathering of wild ingredients has been a life-long interest of mine. I have fond childhood memories of picking wild spring leeks and the sweet wood smoke aroma of the maple sugar shack. I have met several people in our area that gather wild mushrooms as a pastime and have incorporated their ingredients into my menus. Recently I have been learning about the many types of fungi that are in the woods and forests surrounding our resort. The last weekend of August is mushroom pickers' paradise at Resort Tapatoo. Fine edible mushrooms abound. It is our tradition to make mushroom soup on Labour Day Weekend to celebrate nature's bounty.

Using a soft bristled brush remove any soil from wild mushrooms. Do not wash mushrooms in water. This recipe can be made with any mushrooms available in any food store. Please do not attempt picking wild mushrooms unless you are a very experienced mushroom picker.

1 In a four-litre stainless steel saucepot, sweat onion, celery and garlic. Add all mushrooms and cook over medium heat until mushrooms wilt. Add chicken and beef broth, bay leaf, potato and wild rice. Simmer gently, skimming off any foam that develops on surface, until potatoes are tender.

2 Add sherry, parsley and cream, return to simmer. Cornstarch solution may be added at this time if soup is too thin. Consistency should be like hearty chowder.

3 Season with pepper and salt to taste.

4 A tossed salad and any crusty bread on the side makes a nice meal!

YIELD: 8 servings

— *Roy Hintze*

50 grams King Bolete (boletus edulis)

50 grams Slippery Jack (suillus luteus)

50 grams Sidewalk mushroom (agarigus bitorquuis)

50 grams Meadow mushroom (agarigus campestris)

All mushrooms should be thinly sliced.

25 grams butter

50 grams Spanish onion, finely chopped

2 large cloves of garlic, finely chopped

1 large celery stalk, diced finely

1 litre chicken broth

1 litre beef broth

1 large Yukon gold potato diced into bite size cubes

50 grams cooked wild rice

25 ml dry sherry

50 ml 35% cream

25 grams cornstarch dissolved in 25 ml white wine (optional)

2 bay leaves

Freshly chopped parsley

Freshly ground black pepper

Salt

The Ridge at Manitou
Manitouwabing Lake
Parry Sound, Ontario
www.ridgeatmanitou.com
705-389-3978

The Ridge at Manitou

Imagine a private golfing sanctuary where you may see as many moose as birdies. Golf at The Ridge at Manitou is encountered amidst 300 acres of unspoiled nature

surrounding Manitouwabing Lake.

Awarded "Best New Course in Ontario 2005," by Ontario Golf and Fairways magazine, The Ridge is framed by Canadian Shield rock outcroppings and plays through forest and meadowland. Renowned architect Tom McBroom has designed The Ridge to preserve privacy and to inspire and tempt the golfer on every shot.

The course's pristine beauty is matched by the highest standards in hospitality enjoyed in the comfort of our Adirondack-style clubhouse, the heart of club life at The Ridge. Our executive chef, Philip K. Patrick, and his expert culinary team offer an enticing menu of bistro favourites and fresh local fare to be enjoyed while gazing at one of the most spectacular lakeside vistas in Ontario.

PHILIP K. PATRICK, C.C.C.
Executive Chef, The Ridge at Manitou

At The Ridge at Manitou, golf is our priority — but there is so much more, too. The spirit of The Ridge can be experienced in the tasty creations that Philip K. Patrick conjures up in his clubhouse kitchen. Luxurious mussel soup (as featured), fresh local pickerel and a limitless variety of velvety cheesecakes represent the bounty of The Ridge table. Magnificent golf, the magical lakeside vista, summer evenings with stimulating jazz, classical and contemporary music, and fresh seasonal fare are all at the heart of the club's true-north lifestyle. East Coast mussels are a wonderful treat that can be enjoyed as a light meal or a starter for an evening of culinary delight.

Mussel Velouté

A Luxurious Soup with Mediterranean Flavours

1 Rinse mussels in cold water and remove beards.

2 In a kettle bring the water, white wine, Pernod, lemon juice and sea salt to a boil. Add the mussels, steam them, covered, over moderately high heat, stirring once or twice, for 4 to 6 minutes, or until they are opened, and discard any unopened ones.

3 Remove mussels from their shells (keep a few mussels in shells to garnish each portion). Refrigerate mussels until required. Reserve the broth.

4 In a large soup pot, sweat the onions, carrots, fennel, celery and garlic in the olive oil. Add all remaining ingredients (except rice, cream and shelled mussels) and the reserved broth and simmer, covered, for 30 minutes. Add the rice and simmer, covered, for another 40 minutes. Maintain the original level of liquid by adding water and a bit of white wine as necessary.

5 Remove the bay leaves, add shelled mussels and purée the soup until it is very smooth. Return purée to the pot, bring to a gentle boil, then add the cream. Adjust with salt and pepper to taste.

6 Serve with garnish of dill or fennel sprigs and one or two mussels in shells. Enjoy!

YIELD: 6 to 8 servings

— *Philip K. Patrick, C.C.C.*

2 pounds East Coast mussels, tightly closed and fresh

7 cups water or mild fishfumé

1 cup white wine

2 ounces Pernod

½ lemon, juiced

1 teaspoon sea salt

1 large Spanish onion, cut in ½-inch dice

1 Bermuda onion (red), cut in ½-inch dice

3 medium-sized carrots, cut in ½-inch dice

1 medium-sized fennel, cut in thin slices

2 stalks celery, cut in thin slices

1 clove fresh garlic, chopped

1 tablespoon extra virgin olive oil

3 ripe plum tomatoes, chopped

⅓ cup chopped fresh dill

2 bay leaves

¼ teaspoon thyme

¼ teaspoon tarragon

¼ teaspoon basil

¼ teaspoon curry powder

½ teaspoon lemon zest, chopped

Fresh cracked pepper

⅓ cup basmati rice

1 cup 35% whipping cream

NICOLE PETERSON/WWW.PUREIMAGERY.CA

Voice

Alan Bennett, *tenor*
Russell Braun, *baritone,* and Carolyn Maule, *piano*
Mark DuBois, *tenor*
Mary Lou Fallis, *soprano*
Ranee Lee, *jazz vocalist*
Kevin McMillan, *tenor*
Jean Stilwell, *mezzo-soprano*
Veronica Tennant, *dancer/narrator*
Katherine Wheatley, *singer/songwriter*

ALAN BENNETT
Tenor

Lyric tenor Alan Bennett enjoys an active performing, recording, and teaching career. He studied voice at the University of North Carolina and at Indiana University. Alan performs extensively throughout the United States, Canada, South America, and Europe, including performances with many prominent orchestras and conductors. His festival appearances have included the Carmel Bach Festival, Bay Chamber Concerts, the Oregon Bach Festival, and the Tanglewood Festival, as well as the Festival of the Sound. He is on the voice faculty of the Indiana University School of Music.

Dad's Famous Pancakes

My children love the taste of these pancakes, and named them after the cook.

1   Preheat a griddle to 350°F, or heat a skillet over high heat.

2   Sift the flour, cornmeal, and baking powder into a large bowl.

3   In a separate bowl, whisk together the eggs and oil.

4   Add the egg mixture to the dry ingredients along with the milk. Stir the batter until just moistened

5   Drop by ¼ cupfuls onto the hot griddle. Flip when bubbles start to appear on the top, and cook until golden on the bottom.

6   Enjoy with fruit toppings, maple syrup, or whatever you fancy.

YIELD: 12 pancakes

VARIATIONS: Substitute whole wheat flour for half the all-purpose flour, and/or use buttermilk.

— *Alan Bennett*

1½ cups all-purpose flour

1 cup cornmeal*

2 tablespoons baking powder

2 eggs

¼ cup canola oil

2 cups milk

*The fresher the better, preferably from your local mill or farmers' market.

Strawberry Almond Crunch Salad

RUSSELL BRAUN, *Baritone*
CAROLYN MAULE, *Piano*

Russell Braun is one of the most recognized lyric baritones on the international stage today, performing regularly at the Metropolitan Opera, the Salzburg Festival, the Lyric Opera of Chicago, l'Opéra de Paris, and the Canadian Opera Company. He is committed to the song repertoire and is often heard in recital with his wife, pianist Carolyn Maule. Carolyn is a native of Parry Sound who served as page-turner to Festival of the Sound pianists during her own student years. She is one of Canada's most sought-after accompanists, maintaining a busy schedule of concerts, often appearing as a duo with her husband. Carolyn and Russell have two young sons, Benjamin and Gabriel.

Here is a salad that has always met with the approval of family and friends. Thanks to my sister-in-law, Elizabeth Walker-Maule, for introducing it to us!

1 For the almond crunch, in a small skillet over medium heat, stir the almonds, sugar, and water together, stirring frequently until golden brown and crispy, about 10 minutes. Pour the almonds onto a sheet of greased foil. When the nuts are cool enough to handle, break them apart.

2 For the dressing, whisk or shake together in a jar the onion, vegetable oil, vinegar, sugar, poppy seeds (if using), Worcestershire sauce, salt, paprika, and pepper.

3 Place the lettuce and strawberries in a bowl. Just before serving, add the almond crunch and the dressing and toss.

YIELD: 8 servings

— *Russell Braun and Carolyn Maule*

1 head romaine lettuce
(or spinach or mixed salad greens)

2 cups sliced strawberries or raspberries

ALMOND CRUNCH:

½ cup slivered almonds

¼ cup (or less) sugar

2 tablespoons water

DRESSING:

1 small onion, minced

½ cup vegetable oil

¼ cup raspberry vinegar

2 tablespoons sugar

2 tablespoons poppy seeds (optional)

½ teaspoon Worcestershire sauce

½ teaspoon salt

¼ teaspoon paprika

Pepper to taste

JOHANNES IVKOVITZ

Mark's Chicken Mulligatawny

MARK DuBOIS
Tenor

Mark DuBois has been universally acclaimed for the exceptional clarity and tonal purity of his lyric-tenor voice and for his versatility, which allows him to perform opera, operetta, oratorio, lieder, baroque, and musical theatre. He has performed as guest soloist with every major symphony orchestra in Canada and many in the United States. Career highlights include performing for the late Pope John Paul II, Queen Elizabeth II, President Ronald Reagan, and Prime Minister Brian Mulroney.

1 In a large pot, combine the potatoes, coconut milk, water, pepper, salt, coriander, cumin, turmeric, mustard seed, cloves, and peppercorns.

2 Prick the chicken pieces all over with a fork and add them to the pot. The chicken should be nearly covered with the liquid. Add water if necessary.

3 Bring to a boil, and boil for 5 minutes, stirring occasionally. Reduce the heat to low and simmer, uncovered and stirring occasionally, for 25 minutes, or until the chicken is cooked through.

4 In a large skillet, heat the oil over medium-high heat. Fry the onion and garlic, stirring constantly, until browned. Stir into the chicken mixture.

5 Remove from the heat and stir in the chili flakes (if using). Let stand for 1 hour.

6 Reheat the mulligatawny on medium-high heat. Just before serving, stir in the lemon juice. Serve garnished with the cilantro.

7 Serve with basmati rice, chapatis (Indian bread), or pita bread, and raita (cucumber condiment).

YIELD: 4 to 6 servings

— *Mark DuBois*

2 large potatoes, cubed

3 cups coconut milk

3 cups water

2 tablespoons cracked peppercorns

2 tablespoons salt, or to taste

2 tablespoons ground coriander

2 teaspoons ground cumin

1 teaspoon turmeric

1 teaspoon ground mustard seed

½ teaspoon ground cloves

6 peppercorns

15 chicken pieces (drumsticks, thighs, and boneless breasts)

2 tablespoons vegetable oil

1 large onion, chopped

4 cloves garlic, chopped

Dried chili flakes to taste (optional)

Juice of 2 large lemons (optional)

Fresh cilantro leaves, for garnish

Cucumber Raita

1   Sprinkle grated cucumbers with salt and let stand for 15 minutes. Squeeze the cucumbers in a sieve or colander, and drain well.

2   In a bowl, stir together the yogurt, cumin, and paprika. Stir in the cucumber. Chill.

3   Garnish with the chopped parsley and serve with any variety of curries or mulligatawny as a condiment.

— *María DuBois*

2 or 3 cucumbers, grated (with or without skin)

½ teaspoon salt

2 cups yogurt

1 teaspoon ground cumin

½ teaspoon paprika

Chopped fresh parsley, for garnish

Primadonna's Lasagna

MARY LOU FALLIS
Soprano

Mary Lou Fallis holds a unique position in Canada as the country's foremost musical comedienne. She made her operatic debut at 15 years of age as the Second Spirit in a CBC Television production of Mozart's *The Magic Flute.* Known to millions of CBC listeners across the country for her *Diva Diaries,* and to thousands of theatregoers for her *Primadonna* series of one-woman shows, Mary Lou Fallis has single-handedly reinvented the classical music-comedy genre.

I always find myself singing arias while preparing this dish!

1   In a large saucepan, combine the tomatoes, tomato sauce, oregano, and 2 teaspoons of the salt. Start this simmering, uncovered.

2   In a large skillet over medium-high heat, sauté the onions and garlic in the olive oil. Add the ground beef and the remaining 2 teaspoons salt, and cook, stirring frequently, until the meat is no longer pink. Add the beef mixture to the tomato sauce. Simmer, uncovered and stirring occasionally, for 2½ hours.

3   Preheat the oven to 350°F.

4   To a large pot of boiling salted water, add the lasagna noodles and vegetable oil. Cook until noodles are al dente. Drain and separate the noodles.

5   Combine the cheeses.

6   In two 12 by 8 by 2½-inch baking dishes, spread a thin layer of the sauce. Top with one-third of the noodles, then one-third of the combined cheeses, then one-third of the sauce. Repeat this procedure twice, arranging the next layer of noodles in the opposite direction to the first layer. Sprinkle the top layer of sauce with Parmesan cheese.

7   Bake for 40 minutes, or until bubbly. Let stand for 10 minutes before serving.

YIELD: 16 servings

— *Mary Lou Fallis*

2 (28-ounce/796 mL) cans Italian-style tomatoes, chopped, with their juice

2 (14-ounce/398 mL) cans tomato sauce

3 teaspoons dried oregano

4 teaspoons salt

⅓ cup olive oil

2 cups minced onions

2 cloves garlic, minced

2 pounds lean ground beef

¾ pound lasagna noodles

2 tablespoons vegetable oil

¾ pound ricotta cheese (1½ cups)

⅓ pound mozzarella cheese, grated or broken into pieces (1½ cups)

½ pound freshly grated Parmesan cheese (2¼ cups), plus additional for sprinkling

Sweet Potato Soufflé

RANEE LEE
Jazz vocalist

A native of Brooklyn, New York, Ranee Lee began her professional stage career as a dancer. She moved on to playing drums and tenor saxophone with various touring groups in the United States and Canada. After she settled in Montreal 35 years ago, her singing took over and she became one of Canada's most popular jazz vocalists. Ranee is an excellent and highly respected educator. In 1994 she received the International Association of Jazz Educators Award for outstanding service to jazz education and she has been an influential component of the McGill University Faculty of Music for 14 years

I generally serve this dish at Thanksgiving and Christmas, when the entire family comes to visit and eat together. This is one of the recipes that I grew up with. My mom was an excellent cook, and because of her I just love to cook for these occasions. It's like music. You get to combine interesting and fun ideas for everyone to enjoy, and to feel good. We share in the expression that good food feeds the body, and music feeds the soul. We are all the better for it. You will delight the taste buds and sweet tooth of every individual who partakes in this heavenly dish.

1 Preheat the oven to 300°F. Butter a 3-quart casserole dish.

2 Combine the potatoes, honey, butter, and egg yolk. Beat the mixture until fluffy.

3 In a separate bowl, stir together the milk, brown sugar, salt, mace, and nutmeg. Add this slowly to the sweet potato mixture, beating constantly.

4 Beat the egg whites until they stand in stiff peaks, and fold them gently into the sweet potato mixture.

5 Turn the mixture into the buttered casserole and bake for 30 to 35 minutes, or until lightly browned and well puffed. Serve immediately.

YIELD: 8 servings

VARIATION: If you have 12 grandchildren, as Richard and I have, or more or less, they will appreciate this. Preheat the broiler. Spread a layer of miniature marshmallows over the soufflé and broil for as long as it takes to lightly melt and brown the marshmallows (less than 1 minute).

— *Ranee Lee*

4 cups hot cooked mashed sweet potatoes (about 2½ pounds raw)

¼ cup honey

4 tablespoons butter

1 egg yolk

1 (5-ounce) can evaporated milk

2 tablespoons brown sugar

1 teaspoon salt

½ teaspoon mace

¼ teaspoon nutmeg

2 egg whites

Russian Beef Borscht

KEVIN McMILLAN
Tenor

Kevin McMillan is one of Canada's most respected singers and vocal pedagogues, with a career spanning 15 years with almost 700 concerts, 15 recordings, Grammy and Gramophone awards, and numerous Juno nominations. He has appeared with virtually every major North American orchestra and has established a presence in Europe with appearances in the major concert halls of London, Berlin, Barcelona, Hamburg, and Prague. Kevin McMillan is currently an adjunct professor of voice in the Don Wright Faculty of Music at the University of Western Ontario.

I have always liked borscht, although I have no Russian roots. This recipe works really well. It makes heaps, and it's great for cold winter weekends at our cottage on Lake Erie. The flavour of this soup improves with reheating, and leftovers can be frozen.

1 Combine beef broth with enough water to measure 12 cups. Set aside.

2 In a large skillet over medium-high heat, brown the beef quickly. Transfer it to a very large soup kettle. Do not clean the skillet.

3 To the beef, add the broth and water, tomato paste, salt, and white and black pepper. Bring to a boil, reduce the heat, cover, and simmer for 1½ hours, or until the meat is very tender.

4 Meanwhile, in the skillet, heat the oil over medium-high heat. Add the garlic and onions; sauté for 5 minutes. Add the onion mixture to the soup. Add the beets, cabbage, carrots, celery, parsley, dill, dill seed, celery seed, bay leaves, and sugar. Bring the soup back to a boil, reduce the heat, and simmer, uncovered, for 45 minutes, or until the vegetables are tender. Stir in the lemon juice. Discard bay leaves before serving.

5 Offer plain yogurt or sour cream as a topping (unless this is to be a kosher meal), and serve with pumpernickel or rye bread or rolls.

YIELD: 12 servings

— *Kevin McMillan*

2 (10-ounce/284 mL) cans beef broth

1 pound lean beef, cut in ½-inch cubes

1 (5½-ounce/156 mL) can tomato paste

1 teaspoon salt

½ teaspoon white pepper

½ teaspoon black pepper

1 tablespoon vegetable oil

3 large cloves garlic, minced

2 large onions, sliced (2 cups)

4 cups coarsely shredded beets

4 cups coarsely shredded cabbage

2 cups coarsely shredded carrots

1½ cups thinly sliced celery

¼ cup minced fresh parsley (or 2 tablespoons dried parsley flakes)

1½ teaspoons dried dill

1 teaspoon dill seed

1 teaspoon celery seed

2 bay leaves

1½ teaspoons sugar

2 to 4 tablespoons fresh lemon juice, or to taste

Newfoundland Outport Bread

JEAN STILWELL
Mezzo-soprano

Jean Stilwell, hailed on three continents for her complex portrayal of Carmen, is at the forefront of this generation's mezzo-sopranos. Since first assuming the role in Vancouver, Bizet's fascinating gypsy has opened many doors for Jean, and she has appeared with the Buxton Festival, New York City Opera, Welsh National Opera, English National Opera, Opera Zuid of Holland, Pittsburgh Opera, and all the major opera companies of Canada. Jean is the official spokesperson for the ALS Society of Canada and Beatrice House.

When Jean Stilwell came to the Festival of the Sound in 2003, she was invited to submit a recipe for this cookbook. After insisting that she never cooks and that she couldn't possibly offer a recipe, she came up with another idea and asked us to publish this bread recipe. Don Inkpen, a Festival of the Sound Board member, picked Jean up in Toronto and became her friend on the drive to Parry Sound. During her stay, he took her a loaf of Newfoundland Outport Bread, a treat that he has been enjoying since his childhood in Newfoundland. Our tester reports that her biggest problem was refraining from eating a whole loaf while it was still warm.

1 Dissolve the sugar and salt in the water.

2 Put 7 cups of the flour into a very large bowl (with a capacity of more than 14 cups). Sprinkle the yeast over the flour. Add the eggs and melted margarine to the flour. Pour in the warm water. Stir with a large wooden spoon until a consistent slurry is formed. Let the slurry stand for 5 to 10 minutes to allow the yeast to begin working.

3 Slowly add the remaining flour, ½ cup at a time, stirring with a wooden spoon at first, then by hand, until the dough has a consistency that is still moist but does not stick to your hand. It may take less than 7 cups or slightly more depending on the kind of flour, the humidity, and the temperature of the room.

4 Knead the bread, the harder the better, until it is elastic and holds together well. A good way to knead the bread is to punch it as flat as possible, then fold the edges up and to the centre, then punch it down again.

(continued on next page)

¼ cup sugar

2 tablespoons salt

5 cups very warm water

14 cups all-purpose flour (approximate)

2 tablespoons active dry yeast

2 eggs, lightly beaten

½ cup margarine, melted

5 Place the dough in a large bowl, cover with a damp tea towel, and let it rise in a warm place until doubled, 2 or 3 hours.

6 Punch down and knead the dough again. Allow to rise another hour.

7 Generously grease 5 loaf pans with margarine or shortening. Knead the dough a third time, shape it into 5 loaves, and put the loaves into the bread pans. Allow the dough to rise in the pans, covered, for about 45 minutes.

8 Meanwhile, preheat the oven to 425°F.

9 Bake the loaves for 15 minutes. Lower the temperature to 375°F and bake for an additional 17 minutes, until the loaves sound hollow when rapped.

10 Turn the loaves out on dry tea towels and let cool for 2 or more hours. If you prefer a soft crust, brush on some margarine after removing the bread from the oven.

YIELD: 5 loaves

— *Jean Stilwell*

VERONICA TENNANT
Dancer/Narrator

Veronica Tennant was the Prima Ballerina with the National Ballet of Canada for 25 years. She won hearts and accolades performing with the greats, including Erik Bruhn, Rudolf Nureyev, and Mikhail Baryshnikov. An actor, narrator, and gifted communicator, Veronica Tennant has become an internationally recognized filmmaker, director/producer, and writer, with her works garnering several Gemini Awards and the prestigious International Emmy Award. Veronica Tennant was the first dancer to be appointed to the Order of Canada as Officer in 1975, and in 2004 was elevated for the contribution and range of her artistic achievements to the rank of Companion.

Ratatouille

This ratatouille is delicious with pork or beef, and is even better cold the next day. Enjoy!

1   Heat the olive oil in a large skillet over medium-high heat. Sauté the garlic and onion until they become a deep, golden brown.

2   In a small dish, combine the sugar and soy sauce.

3   In a large microwave-safe casserole dish (glass is nice to show the layers), layer one-third of the onion mixture and top with one-third of the eggplant. Sprinkle with one-third of the soy sauce mixture, and top with one-third of the tomatoes. Press down on the layers gently. Repeat the layers two more times, pushing the layers down as you go. Pour the reserved tomato juice on top. Sprinkle with the herbs.

4   Microwave on high until the ratatouille is heated through, 30 to 40 minutes. Serve immediately.

YIELD: 4 servings

— *Veronica Tennant*

3 tablespoons olive oil

2 cloves garlic, minced

1 small Vidalia onion, chopped

3 tablespoons sugar

1 tablespoon soy sauce

3 small baby eggplants, unpeeled, thinly sliced

4 cups chopped fresh plum tomatoes (reserving juice) or 1 (28-ounce/796 mL) can Italian plum tomatoes, chopped (juices reserved)

Handful roughly chopped fresh herbs (basil, thyme, oregano)

BRUCE ZINGER

Crab Cakes

KATHERINE WHEATLEY
Singer/songwriter

Singer and songwriter Katherine Wheatley grew up in Parry Sound. She graduated from Queen's University with a geology degree and spent five seasons roughing it in the bush, gathering not only rock samples but material for her songs. It was only a matter of time before she left her tent and recorded her first CD. Her passion for songwriting began with a $13 guitar ordered from the Sears catalogue. Katherine has become a regular at folk festivals, concert series, and clubs across Canada.

I collected this recipe, along with the Nova Scotia Scallop and Spinach Soup recipe, while on tour on the East Coast.

1 In a large bowl, combine the crab, bread crumbs, vegetable mixture, parsley, salt, and pepper.

2 In a separate bowl, beat the egg. Stir in the mayonnaise, lemon juice, Worcestershire sauce, Dijon mustard, and Tabasco sauce.

3 Add mayonnaise mixture to the crab mixture, mix well with your hands, and shape into 10 to 12 patties.

4 Heat the oil in a large nonstick skillet over medium-high heat. Fry the crab cakes, turning once, until lightly golden on both sides, about 5 minutes each side. Serve hot with tartar sauce.

YIELD: 10 to 12 medium cakes

— *Katherine Wheatley*

2 (7-ounce/198 gram) cans good-quality crab (or 1 pound frozen crab)

1½ cups fresh bread crumbs

1 cup mixed finely diced onion, celery, and green pepper (about ⅓ cup each)

1 tablespoon finely chopped fresh parsley

Salt and pepper to taste

1 egg

¾ cup mayonnaise

1 tablespoon freshly squeezed lemon juice

½ teaspoon Worcestershire sauce

½ teaspoon Dijon mustard

Tabasco sauce to taste

1 tablespoon vegetable oil

Fresh Strawberry Pie

This tasty summer recipe is from my mother.

1   In a bowl, crush half the strawberries with a potato masher (use up any imperfect ones first). Set aside the remaining strawberries.

2   Combine the sugar and cornstarch in a small saucepan. Add the crushed strawberries and the water. Cook over medium heat, stirring gently, until the juice is thick and clear.

3   Remove from the heat and stir in the Cointreau, butter, lemon juice, and orange zest, stirring until the butter has melted. Let the glaze cool 5 minutes.

4   Arrange the remaining whole strawberries in the pie shell. Pour the cooled glaze over top. Chill thoroughly.

5   Top with whipped cream before serving.

YIELD: approximately 8 servings

— *Katherine Wheatley*

1 quart fresh strawberries

1 cup sugar

3 tablespoons cornstarch

½ cup water

2 tablespoons Cointreau or other orange liqueur

1 tablespoon unsalted butter

1 tablespoon freshly squeezed lemon juice

Freshly grated orange zest to taste

1 baked 9-inch pie shell

Slightly sweetened whipped cream

Nova Scotia Scallop and Spinach Soup

I collected this recipe, along with the Crab Cakes recipe, while on tour on the East Coast.

1   Melt the butter in a heavy saucepan over medium heat. Add the bell pepper and onion, and sauté until almost tender, about 3 minutes.

2   Add the chicken stock, spinach, cream, and chili flakes. Cover and simmer until the spinach is tender, about 3 minutes. Stir in the scallops and simmer, uncovered, until scallops are just opaque in the centre, about 3 minutes.

3   Stir in the basil. Season with salt and pepper. Serve immediately.

YIELD: 2 to 4 servings

— *Katherine Wheatley*

2 tablespoons unsalted butter

½ cup diced red bell pepper

½ cup finely chopped onion

2 cups chicken stock

1½ cups packed sliced spinach

¼ cup heavy cream

A pinch of dried chili flakes

10 ounces sea scallops, halved horizontally, or whole bay scallops

3 tablespoons chopped fresh basil

Salt and pepper to taste

Winds

David Bourque, *bass clarinet*
The Canadian Tribute to Glenn Miller
Guy Few, *trumpet*
The Hannaford Street Silver Band
Susan Hoeppner, *flute*
Brian James, *oboe*
Ian McDougall, *trombone*
James McKay, *bassoon*
Harvey Seigel, *trombone*
Suzanne Shulman, *flute*
Rick Wilkins, *saxophone*
Thomas Wolf, *flute*

CBC Yams

DAVID BOURQUE
Bass clarinet

David Bourque has been the
bass clarinetist in the Toronto
Symphony Orchestra since 1983.
He has also played bass clarinet
with many other Canadian
orchestras, including the National
Ballet, the Canadian Opera
Company, the Stratford Festival,
the National Arts Centre, and
the Montreal Symphony. He is
active in film and television sound
recording, including a performance
for the film score of the Academy
Award–winning Norman Jewison
film, *Moonstruck.* He is also an
avid golfer. David Bourque is
an adjunct assistant professor
at the Faculty of Music, University
of Toronto.

*I picked up this unusual recipe from "The Vicki Gabereau Show"
on CBC Radio. It's a great fall and winter dish. The bananas add a
distinctive but not readily identifiable flavour to this savoury comfort
food. If you don't have a ripe banana, mash an unripe one and let it
sit out for a couple of hours.*

1   Pierce each yam all over with a fork. Microwave the
yams on high for 15 minutes. Turn the yams over and
cook until tender, about 12 minutes longer. (Or you
can bake them in the oven at 375°F for 45 minutes.)
Cool. Cut the yams in half, and scoop the pulp into
a food processor. Purée.

2   Add the banana, sour cream, orange juice and
zest, cinnamon, cloves, ginger, nutmeg, and mace
(if using). (Feel free to add a greater quantity of
the spices to taste. The more the merrier. More sour
cream won't hurt either.) Stir until well combined.
Stir in the green onions gently so as not to mash
them. Transfer the mixture to a casserole dish.
(The yams can be kept in the refrigerator for
1 to 2 days to blend the flavours, if desired.)

3   Preheat the oven to 350°F.

4   Reheat the yams in the oven, covered, for
30 minutes. Garnish with the almonds and
cinnamon, and heat, uncovered, an additional
15 minutes.

YIELD: 4 to 6 servings

— *David Bourque*

3 or 4 large fresh yams or
sweet potatoes

1 ripe banana, mashed

2 tablespoons sour cream

2 tablespoons orange juice

2 tablespoons orange zest

½ teaspoon cinnamon

¼ teaspoon ground cloves

¼ teaspoon ground ginger

¼ teaspoon nutmeg

A few dashes of mace
(optional)

2 tablespoons chopped
green onion

Sliced almonds and
cinnamon, for garnish

Spicy Eggplant

1 Preheat the oven to 350°F.

2 Cut the ends off the eggplant, and slice the eggplant diagonally. Toss the eggplant slices with 2½ tablespoons of the oil, and place them on a nonstick baking sheet in a single layer. Bake for 15 minutes, or until the eggplant is very soft, turning the slices once halfway through cooking.

3 Heat the remaining 2½ tablespoons oil in a wok over medium-high heat. Add the pork, and stir-fry until it is no longer pink (do not overcook).

4 Add the green onions, garlic, ginger, and chili paste. Stir-fry for 30 seconds or so, until fragrant.

5 Add the eggplant, sake, soy sauce, Worcestershire sauce, and sugar. Stir-fry for 1 minute or so, until the eggplant is hot. Adjust seasoning, adding more chili paste, sake, soy sauce, or Worcestershire sauce as needed. Add salt sparingly to taste.

6 Stir in the cornstarch, dissolved in a small amount of cold water or other liquid, to thicken the sauce, if desired.

7 Serve immediately.

YIELD: 3 to 4 servings

— *David Bourque*

1½ pounds Japanese eggplant (approximately 3 eggplants)

5 tablespoons peanut oil or vegetable oil

½ pound ground pork

3 green onions, coarsely chopped

1 or 2 cloves garlic, finely chopped

2 tablespoons finely chopped fresh ginger

2 teaspoons chili paste (sambal oelek) or bean paste with chili

1 teaspoon sake (Japanese rice wine)

1 teaspoon soy sauce

1 teaspoon Worcestershire sauce

½ teaspoon white or brown sugar

Salt

Cornstarch, for thickening

Hot Crabmeat Dip

This is my favourite appetizer. The band calls it a real winner.

1 Preheat the oven to 350°F.

2 Combine all the ingredients and mix well. Turn the mixture into a pie plate or small casserole dish. Bake for 15 minutes.

3 Serve warm or at room temperature with crackers or chips.

YIELD: serves about 16

— *Don Pierre*

2 (8-ounce) packages cream cheese

2 (7½-ounce) cans crabmeat, picked over

6 tablespoons mayonnaise

2 tablespoons each chopped red and green peppers

2 tablespoons chopped green onion

1 tablespoon Worcestershire sauce

1 tablespoon lemon juice

½ teaspoon horseradish

½ teaspoon dry mustard

THE CANADIAN TRIBUTE TO GLENN MILLER
Big Band

The Canadian Tribute to Glenn Miller, under the direction of Don Pierre, manages to effectively stop the world and transport audiences back to the early '40s, back to the war years, the all-important radio broadcasts, the big dance halls. Great pains have been taken to recreate the distinctive Miller sound with an outstanding 22-piece orchestra and vocal quartet. Instrumental and vocal arrangements were gleaned note-for-note from original recordings: the timing, phrasing, instrumentation, and "muted" sound is all Glenn Miller.

Guy's Heart Attack Potatoes

GUY FEW
Trumpet

Guy Few is a virtuoso. As a powerful pianist and astonishing trumpeter, he delights audiences with his intensity and charm. He has appeared with all of Canada's major orchestras and at the most prestigious concert halls. Guy is a gold medal graduate of Wilfrid Laurier University and holds a Fellowship Diploma from Trinity College, London, England. He has been invited as a professor, soloist, principal, or recitalist to many festivals. Guy is a faculty member at Wilfrid Laurier University, teaching trumpet and duo piano and conducting the Wilfrid Laurier Brass Ensemble.

I am one of those cooks that makes things up. I have been cooking and baking for many years, and I seem to have a handle on my way to put things together. As a result, these recipes may be too weird for you guys—but do whatever makes you happy. Just be sure to have emergency services on speed dial!

1 Preheat the oven to 350°F. Grease the bottom of a large casserole with olive oil.

2 Boil the potatoes in salted water; drain. Whip the potatoes with the butter, cream, garlic, salt and pepper.

3 Toast the bread. Grind it in a food processor with the Parmesan cheese, sage, and black pepper to taste.

4 Cover the bottom of the casserole with one-third of the crumb mixture. Layer with half of the potatoes and then with half of the cheddar. Repeat the layers, finishing with the remaining crumbs on the top. Sprinkle with Parmesan and cheddar.

5 Bake the potatoes, uncovered, for 30 minutes, or until they are heated through.

YIELD: 10 to 12 servings

— *Guy Few*

12 good-sized potatoes, peeled

Butter to taste

Heavy cream to taste

Garlic cloves to taste, minced

Salt and freshly ground pepper to taste

3 slices multi-grain bread

About ⅓ cup grated Parmesan cheese, plus a little extra for topping

1 teaspoon powdered sage

½ pound shredded cheddar cheese, plus a little extra for topping

Mocha Truffle Cake

This is a real recipe that I have altered. It is very popular in chocolate circles. If this is on the same menu as the "heart attack potatoes," you should definitely check yourself immediately afterwards into a good heart clinic!

1 Preheat the oven to 350°F. Line the bottom and sides of a 10-inch springform cake pan with foil, allowing the foil to extend 1 inch above the rim of the pan. Coat the foil with some of the butter, and smooth out the foil.

2 In a saucepan, combine the chocolate, the remaining butter, the sugar, and espresso. Bring to a simmer over low heat, stirring until the sugar dissolves. Remove from the heat and let cool.

3 Beat the eggs until thick. Stir them into the chocolate mixture. Pour the batter into the cake pan.

4 Bake for 50 minutes, or until the centre is just set (it won't jiggle if you gently shake the pan).

5 Cool completely in the pan. Cover the cake and refrigerate it in the pan until firm, at least 8 hours.

6 A few hours before serving this cake, whip the cream with the superfine sugar, cocoa powder, and vanilla.

7 Invert the cake onto a serving platter, and ice it with the whipped mixture. Decorate with the dragées and violets. (You could also use chocolate flakes or curls, or nuts, or whatever you like.)

YIELD: 10 to 12 servings

— *Guy Few*

---

1 pound butter, cut into pieces

1 pound good-quality dark chocolate, chopped

2 cups granulated sugar

1 cup espresso or strong coffee

8 large eggs, at room temperature

1 cup heavy cream

¼ cup superfine sugar

¼ cup good-quality cocoa powder

¼ teaspoon vanilla

Silver dragées and candied violets, for garnish

Salmon in Soy Sauce and Maple Syrup

This makes a great, easy summer meal.

1   In a nonreactive baking dish or resealable plastic bag, mix together the soy sauce, maple syrup, herbes de Provence, and pepper. Add the salmon, coating with the marinade, and marinate, refrigerated, for 4 to 8 hours.

2   Remove the salmon from the marinade, reserving the marinade. Cook the salmon in any way that makes you happy—bake, broil, or barbecue.

3   Meanwhile, simmer the marinade until slightly thickened and reduced.

4   Whisk together the olive oil and balsamic vinegar in a 3-to-1 ratio, or to taste.

5   Toss the greens with the blue cheese, walnut pieces, and dressing. Divide the salad among 4 plates, top with the salmon, and drizzle the salmon with the reduced marinade.

YIELD: 4 servings

— *Guy Few*

1 cup soy sauce

1 cup maple syrup

A pinch of herbes de Provence

Black pepper to taste

4 portions of salmon fillet

Olive oil

Balsamic vinegar

Mixed greens (enough for 4 people)

¼ cup blue cheese, crumbled

Walnut pieces

Hannaford Goulash

THE HANNAFORD STREET SILVER BAND
Brass Band

The Hannaford Street Silver Band is Canada's award-winning premier professional brass band and Resident Company of Toronto's St. Lawrence Centre for the Arts. Since 1983, the Hannaford Street Silver Band has been striking up the brass band tradition and stirring up critical and popular acclaim. The band maintains a vigorous commissioning program, resulting in new concert works for bands. In recognition of its accomplishments, the band was awarded its second Lieutenant Governor's Award for the Arts in November 2003.

This typical Hungarian meal is known worldwide and is a favourite of gourmets who like complicated yet characteristic tastes. This stew, which is enhanced by its fiery red colour, should be rich and thick, as it is a typical one-course meal. A beloved food of the Hannaford and Black Dyke Bands, it just keeps going and going and going . . .

1   Cut the pork and beef into ½-inch cubes. Rinse thoroughly and dry on paper towels.

2   Heat the oil in a large saucepan over medium-high heat. Sauté the onions until golden. Take the saucepan off the heat. Sprinkle on the paprika and quickly stir. Add 2 tablespoons water. Put the saucepan back on the heat, and boil the mixture to reduce it until most of the liquid is evaporated.

3   Reduce the heat to medium-low. Add the pork, beef, sausage, and salt. Stir well. Cover and simmer gently until the meat is browned. Stir in the cumin, garlic, and bay leaves. Braise for 10 minutes, adding a little water if the mixture seems dry, until the meat has picked up the flavour of the seasonings.

4   In the meantime, peel the potatoes and cut them into ½-inch cubes; set them aside in a bowl of cold water. Slice the green pepper and tomato. Set aside.

5   To make the noodles, combine the flour and salt in a bowl. Stir in the egg, then gradually work in enough water to make a stiff dough. Pinch off marble-sized pieces of dough and place them in a floured bowl.

(continued on next page)

1 pound pork shank

1 pound beef shank

⅓ cup vegetable oil

2 large onions, finely chopped

2½ tablespoons sweet Hungarian paprika

1 pound smoked Hungarian sausage

2 teaspoons salt (or less)

¼ teaspoon ground cumin

2 cloves garlic, minced

2 bay leaves

4 medium new potatoes

1 green pepper

1 tomato

4 cups water

Finely chopped hot cherry pepper to taste

Sour cream, for garnish

6 Cook the noodles in a pot of boiling salted water until tender. Drain and rinse under cold water. (You could buy gnocchi if you don't want to make the noodles, but the flag would fly upside down!)

7 When the meat is almost tender, drain the potatoes and add them to the goulash along with the green pepper and water. Reduce heat to low and simmer for a few minutes. Bring to a boil, then reduce heat, add the tomato, and simmer until the meat and potatoes are tender. Discard the bay leaves.

8 Add the noodles, and simmer for 3 minutes or until the noodles are heated through.

9 Add salt and cherry pepper to your liking.

10 Serve hot, with a dollop of sour cream.

YIELD: 6 to 8 servings

— *Hannaford Street Silver Band*

NOODLES:

½ cup all-purpose flour

⅛ teaspoon salt

1 egg, lightly beaten

Apricot-Dijon Lamb with Rosemary and Baked Vegetables

SUSAN HOEPPNER
Flute

Canadian flutist Susan Hoeppner is in great demand as an international solo recitalist and chamber musician. Early in her career Susan was the Grand Prize Winner of the Canadian Music Competition, the first woodwind player ever to receive this honour in the competition's history. She went on to win the CBC Young Performer's Competition and first prize in the Olga Koussevitsky Competition for Woodwinds held at the Lincoln Center in New York City. She is also heralded by James Galway as "one of the best talents of her generation."

The following is a no-fail, sure-win recipe.

1 Preheat the oven to 425°F.

2 Cut the cauliflower into large florets. Cut the red and green peppers into long strips. In a small bowl, stir together ¼ cup of the olive oil, 1 tablespoon of the rosemary, the chili flakes, salt, and pepper. Toss the oil mixture with the vegetables and arrange the vegetables in a single layer on a baking sheet. Roast for about 25 minutes, until tender and crisp.

3 In a small bowl, stir together the apricot jam, mustard, and remaining 2 tablespoons rosemary.

4 In a large skillet, heat the remaining 1 tablespoon olive oil over medium heat. Brown the lamb chops for 7 to 10 minutes per side for medium-rare. Turn the heat down to medium-low. Add the jam mixture and simmer for 10 minutes.

5 Meanwhile, rinse the rice under cold running water. Combine the rice, stock, and salt in a 3-quart saucepan that has a tight-fitting lid. Bring to a boil, stirring once or twice. Lower heat to a simmer. Cover and cook for 18 minutes, without removing the lid or stirring.

6 Sprinkle the rice with chopped parsley, and serve the lamb chops with the rice and baked vegetables.

YIELD: 2 servings

— *Susan Hoeppner*

½ cauliflower

1 each red and green pepper

¼ cup plus 1 tablespoon olive oil

3 tablespoons finely chopped fresh rosemary

½ teaspoon dried chili flakes

Salt and pepper to taste

2 tablespoons each apricot jam and Dijon mustard (or more, depending on the size of the chops)

4 lamb chops

1 cup long-grain or basmati rice

2 cups chicken stock

Chopped fresh parsley

Bubba's F. G. Chili

BRIAN JAMES
Oboe

Brian James was raised in a musical family in Alexandria, Virginia. His father (an oboist), his mother (a choral director), his stepfather (a French hornist), and his stepmother (a singer) all supported him and encouraged him to pursue his own musical career playing the oboe. Brian is the second oboe and English horn with Symphony Nova Scotia. During the summer seasons Brian has performed with such festivals as the Festival of the Sound, the Orford Music Festival, the Edinburgh Festival, the Brevard Music Festival, the Todi Opera Festival, and the Grand River Baroque Festival.

This recipe came from a wonderful mother of a wonderful roommate of mine in Pittsburgh during my master's days. The Old Bay Seasoning is my addition. It was a staple seasoning for the crabs I grew up eating every summer in Maryland. It's a nice touch if you can find it. I have seen it in a grocery store in Collingwood. So there is hope. Look in the seasonings section or in a fish store. The cinnamon is the key to the sweet Cincinnati-style taste.

This recipe produces a fairly thick chili that will last quite a while, only getting better from day to day. It's great with sweet cornbread and beer! Of course, any meat can be added for all you carnivores.

1   Put the crushed tomatoes in a large pot over low heat. Add the carrots, potatoes, and onion and simmer for 10 minutes. Then add the red and green peppers and garlic; simmer for another 10 minutes. Add the canned beans, corn, peanuts, cashews, chili powder, Old Bay Seasoning, cinnamon, salt and black pepper. Simmer, uncovered and stirring occasionally, over low heat for as long as you like to allow the flavours to blend.

YIELD: 6 generous servings

— *Brian James*

2 (28-ounce/796 mL) cans crushed tomatoes

2 carrots, chopped

4 red potatoes, diced

1 red onion, chopped

1 each red and green pepper, chopped

2 to 4 cloves garlic, minced

1 (14-ounce/398 mL) can pinto beans, drained and rinsed

1 (14-ounce/398 mL) can black beans, drained and rinsed

1 (14-ounce/398 mL) can kidney beans, drained and rinsed

1 (14-ounce/398 mL) can corn, drained

½ cup unsalted roasted peanuts

½ cup cashews

Chili powder to taste

Old Bay Seasoning to taste

Cinnamon to taste

Salt and black pepper to taste

Eeny's Rack of Lamb
(Paucity of Mountain Goats, aka Lack of Ram)

IAN McDOUGALL
Trombone

Ian McDougall was born in Calgary and grew up in Victoria, leaving there in 1960 to tour in Great Britain with the John Dankworth Band. He returned to Canada in 1962 and began a lengthy career as a freelance player, composer, and arranger in Vancouver and in Toronto, where, until 1991, he was also the lead and solo trombonist with Rob McConnell's award-winning Boss Brass. Ian now resides once again in Victoria, where he teaches trombone and jazz studies at the University of Victoria.

Our testers say that this rack of lamb was better than any they have eaten in restaurants! Recommended wine: Aussie Shiraz.

1 Preheat the oven to 350°F.

2 Make yourself a dry martini.

3 Remove all excess fat from the lamb with a sharp knife, and season it with salt and pepper.

4 Have a sip of your martini. (Cheers!)

5 In an ovenproof skillet, heat 3 tablespoons of the olive oil. When the oil is hot but not smoking, sear the lamb for about 2 minutes, first on the two flat sides, and then on the bony edge. You may have to hold the rack with tongs while you are searing the edge.

6 Remove the lamb from pan, and allow it to rest on a plate for a few minutes. Meanwhile, drain the oil from the pan. Sip some more martini.

7 In a small bowl, stir together the remaining 1 tablespoon olive oil, the mustard, garlic, rosemary, and lots of sea salt and freshly ground pepper. Coat the lamb with the mustard mixture. Put the lamb back into the skillet, ribs down.

8 Roast the lamb for 15 to 20 minutes. This should result in a perfect medium-rare rack.

YIELD: 2 servings

— Ian McDougall

1 rack of lamb (8 ribs), frenched

Sea salt and freshly ground pepper to taste

4 tablespoons olive oil

2 tablespoons (or more) Dijon mustard

3 cloves garlic, minced

2 or 3 sprigs fresh rosemary, chopped

Classic Baguettes

This is classic French bread with the four French-government-approved ingredients: flour, salt, yeast, and water. Have some for me. My doctor says I have to give up bread until I lose another 20 pounds!

1 In a food processor fitted with the steel blade, combine the warm water, yeast, and salt. Let stand for 5 minutes, until foamy, then stir with a fork. Add the flour and process for 20 seconds, until the dough forms a mass on the blade.

2 Put the dough into a warm floured bowl, cover, and let it rise in a warm place until doubled, about 1 hour. Punch it down, and again let it rise until doubled, 1 hour.

3 Knead the dough on a lightly floured surface, until smooth, elastic, and no longer sticky. Divide the dough into three equal portions. Shape each portion into a long, narrow baguette 20 to 24 inches long.

4 Brush a baking sheet with olive oil. Transfer the baguettes to the baking sheet, cover with a clean dish towel, and let rise until doubled, about 40 minutes.

5 Meanwhile, put a small baking pan on the floor of the oven or on the bottom rack and preheat the oven to 425°F.

6 Just before putting the baguettes in the oven, using a very sharp razor blade (I use an antique straight razor that belonged to my wife's grandfather), cut 4 long diagonal slashes in the top of each loaf. These cuts should be on a very sharp angle, almost parallel to the baguette itself.

7 Toss a couple of handfuls of ice cubes into the hot baking pan to create steam. Bake the bread for 12 minutes, then rotate the baking sheet 180 degrees. At the same time, spray the tops of the loaves and the walls of the oven with water.

8 Bake another 16 minutes or so. Remove a loaf and test by rapping on the bottom with your knuckles. If it's crusty and has a hollow sound, then the bread is ready. If not, bake for another 5 or 6 minutes. Cool on a rack.

YIELD: 3 loaves

— *Ian McDougall*

2 cups warm water

4 teaspoons active dry yeast

2 teaspoons sea salt

4¼ cups flour (white bread flour is best, but all-purpose will do)

Shrimp and Paella

JAMES McKAY
Bassoon

James McKay maintains an active schedule as a bassoonist, conductor, acoustic researcher, university professor, and adjudicator. He has toured throughout the world as a soloist, chamber musician, and conductor. He is the chair of the Department of Music Performance Studies in the Don Wright Faculty of Music at the University of Western Ontario, and is the director of the Reverberation and Acoustics in Performance Studio and lab. He is the Music Director of Symphony Hamilton. Jim is an avid scuba diver and recently was certified as an underwater photographer.

A few years ago at Christmas, my wife bought me a cookbook that featured meals made in a skillet. I had fun with this book and began experimenting with different ingredients. After a few months, I actually made the following dinner for my mother-in-law and wife, and we all survived!

1. Rinse the rice under cold running water and place it in a microwave-safe dish with a lid. Add enough of the stock to cover the rice. Cover and microwave at high for 12 minutes, or until the stock is absorbed.

2. In a large nonstick skillet over medium heat, toast the saffron, stirring frequently, for 2 to 3 minutes. Remove the saffron.

3. In the same skillet, heat the oil over medium heat. Add the shrimp. Cook, stirring frequently, until the shrimp are done, 1 to 2 minutes. Remove the shrimp with a slotted spoon and set them aside.

4. Add the onion and pepper to the oil in the skillet, and cook over medium heat, stirring constantly, until the onion is tender and golden.

5. Return the shrimp to the skillet. Add the saffron and the remaining stock. Gradually stir in the rice as you bring the whole thing gently to a boil. Reduce the heat and simmer, covered, until the liquid has been almost absorbed, about 10 minutes.

6. Stir in the artichoke hearts, peas, and tomato. Season with salt and pepper, and cook for another 3 minutes.

YIELD: 4 to 6 servings

— *Jim McKay (Bassoon Jim)*

2 cups long-grain white rice

4 cups chicken stock (approximate)

¼ teaspoon crushed saffron

2 tablespoons extra virgin olive oil

1 pound medium shrimp, peeled and deveined

1 onion, diced

½ red pepper, diced

1 (14-ounce/398 mL) can artichoke hearts, drained and quartered

1 cup frozen green peas

1 tomato, diced

Salt and pepper to taste

The Tenderest Chicken Recipe

HARVEY SEIGEL
Trombone

Harvey Seigel, vocalist, trombonist, entertainer, and leader of the Fabulous Harvey Seigel Band, performs with Toronto's most talented musicians. The band comprises Canada's finest full-time professional musicians and vocalists. Their intense love for music always ensures spectacular, fun-filled performances.
The band is comfortable with all types of music ranging from the 1920s right up to the present. An evening with the Harvey Seigel Band is always a night to remember.

This is, honestly, THE TENDEREST CHICKEN you will ever experience. If you love the succulent taste of chicken the way you get it at a gourmet Chinese restaurant, you will adore this simple, error-free method of cooking "Chinese chicken," which can then be used in soups, wraps, salads, pastas, sandwiches—whatever you wish.

1   Cut the carrots and celery into medium-sized pieces and place them in a stockpot filled with cold water. Add the garlic, bay leaf, and peppercorns. Bring to a rapid boil and boil for 10 minutes.

2   Place the chicken breasts on top of the ingredients in the pot. Cover the pot and bring the water back to a rapid boil. When the water returns to a rapid boil, turn off the burner, and DO NOT LIFT THE LID AGAIN. Allow the pot's contents to "steep" undisturbed for 20 minutes.

3   At the end of 20 minutes, remove the chicken breasts with a slotted spoon. Cover the chicken with plastic wrap and allow it to cool to room temperature. Then place the chicken breasts in the refrigerator until you require them.

YIELD: 6 servings

— *Harvey Seigel*

3 large carrots

3 stalks celery

2 cloves garlic

1 bay leaf

½ teaspoon black peppercorns

3 large chicken breasts, skin on and bone in (premium chicken works best)

PLEASE—NO SALT AT ALL!

Maureen Forrester's Wild Rice Casserole

SUZANNE SHULMAN
Flute

One of Canada's outstanding instrumentalists, Suzanne Shulman has received critical acclaim for solo recitals at Carnegie Hall, London's Queen Elizabeth Hall and Wigmore Hall, and in the Chopin Institute in Warsaw. She has appeared as a soloist with major Canadian and international orchestras and is a frequent guest at chamber music festivals. Suzanne has premiered works by Jean Coulthard, Christos Hatzis, Srul Irving Glick, and Jacques Hétu and is the flute soloist on all the Classical Kids recordings. She teaches flute at McMaster University.

This recipe is one I have made countless times for post-concert receptions at our home. It is really satisfying for hungry musicians and other guests alike. It's easy to prepare, and goes well with a salad and garlic bread. Thank you to Maureen Forrester!

1. Preheat the oven to 325°F. Grease a large casserole dish.

2. Pour the boiling water over the rice in a large bowl, and let it stand for 25 minutes. Drain the rice and return it to the bowl.

3. Heat the oil in a large skillet over medium-high heat. Add the onion and cook, stirring frequently, until browned. Add the ground beef and cook, stirring frequently, until browned.

4. Add the beef mixture to the rice. Add the mushroom soup, chicken soup, consommé, mushrooms and their liquid, water, poultry seasoning, salt, pepper, celery salt, onion salt, garlic salt, paprika, bay leaf, and parsley. Mix well.

5. Turn the mixture into the casserole, and bake, uncovered, for 3 hours.

6. Near the end of the baking time, sprinkle the almonds over the casserole.

SUGGESTIONS: Assemble the night before and keep covered and refrigerated, for baking the next day. Try substituting leftover turkey for the ground beef. If the recipe seems to be too salty, use low-sodium soups, and use only salt to taste.

YIELD: 10 to 12 servings

— *Suzanne Shulman*

1 cup wild rice

3 cups boiling water

4 tablespoons vegetable oil

6 tablespoons chopped onions

1½ pounds ground beef

1 (10-ounce/284 mL) can condensed cream of mushroom soup

1 (10-ounce/284 mL) can condensed cream of chicken soup

1 (10-ounce/284 mL) can consommé

1 (10-ounce/284 mL) can sliced mushrooms with liquid

1 cup water

1 tablespoon poultry seasoning

½ teaspoon each salt and pepper

¼ teaspoon each celery salt, onion salt, garlic salt, and paprika

1 bay leaf, crumbled

Lots of chopped fresh parsley

½ cup chopped almonds

GADI HOZ

Oriental Pork with Roasted Sweet Potatoes

RICK WILKINS
Tenor saxophone

Rick Wilkins is an arranger, composer, conductor, and tenor saxophonist. His early experience was as a saxophonist and arranger with the dance bands of Jack Ryan and Gav Morton, Benny Louis, and others. He studied arranging briefly with Phil Nimmons at the Advanced School of Contemporary Music and thereafter made his living primarily in that field. He has prepared and often conducted music for CBC and CTV. For CBS TV, Los Angeles, he was music director for a series and several specials starring the singing group the Jackson Five. Rick also scored Oscar Peterson's "Canadiana Suite."

This recipe is delicious and easy to prepare. I have also cooked it in a very heavy pan on the barbecue.

1 Preheat the oven to 450°F. Generously spray or brush a baking sheet with oil.

2 Peel the potato and slice it into wedges no thicker than 1 inch. Toss them in a bowl with the olive oil and salt. Spread them out on the baking sheet, leaving room in the centre for the pork.

3 Trim any fat and membrane from the meat. Make 5 shallow diagonal slashes about ½ inch apart in the top of the pork. Using your hands, rub the pork with the hoisin sauce until it is evenly coated. Place the pork in the centre of the baking sheet, tucking the narrow end of the meat underneath.

4 Roast in the middle of the oven for 25 to 30 minutes, stirring the potatoes occasionally, until an instant-read thermometer inserted in the pork reads 155°F for medium-well done. If the potato wedges are done before the pork is fully cooked, remove them to a large plate and cover loosely with foil.

5 Let the pork stand for 3 minutes before slicing.

YIELD: 2 servings

— *Rick Wilkins*

1 large sweet potato

1 teaspoon olive oil

A pinch of salt

1 pork tenderloin (approximately ¾ pound)

1 tablespoon hoisin sauce

Lubo's Borscht

THOMAS WOLF
Flute

Thomas Wolf comes from a Russian family of musicians where cooking was as essential as music in living a good life. In fact, family feasts and musicales went hand in hand. Tom's greatest culinary achievement was feeding the Serkin family and 150 other musicians a meal of Russian shaslik and other delectables at the Marlboro Music Festival in Vermont in 1965. He has had a distinguished career as musician, educator, consultant, author, and administrator. He was a soloist with the Philadelphia Orchestra at the age of sixteen. A co-founder of Bay Chamber Concerts, he currently serves as its Executive and Artistic Director, and is chair and CEO of Wolf, Keens & Company.

"Lubo" was my grandmother, Lea Luboschutz, a famous violinist from Russia who toured the world during the first third of the twentieth century.

1. Put the shin bone in a stockpot or large Dutch oven and add the V8 juice. Add enough water to just cover the shin bone. Add the onions, bay leaf, peppercorns, and salt. Simmer, covered, until the meat is tender, 2 hours or more.

2. Stir in the cabbage. Continue to cook until the meat falls off the bone and the cabbage is soft, about 1 hour.

3. Remove the pot from the heat and take out the meat and bones. Discard the bones. Cut the meat into bite-sized pieces. Reserve, covered, in the fridge.

4. Cool the broth, preferably overnight, and skim off the fat.

5. Trim the beets, leaving 1 inch of the stems on. Bring to a boil in a pot of water. When beets are soft when pierced with a fork, they are done (30 to 60 minutes). Remove the beets from the pot, reserving the cooking liquid. When the beets are cool enough to handle, slip off the skins, and slice or chop the beets. Add the beets and their cooking liquid to the soup and reheat.

(continued on next page)

1 5-pound beef shin bone

1 (48-ounce/1.3 L) can V8 juice

2 large onions, chopped (1 to 2 cups)

1 bay leaf

A handful of peppercorns

Salt to taste

1 large green cabbage (or 2 small ones), cored and shredded

4 bunches beets

1 (5½-ounce/156 mL) can tomato paste

Juice of 3 or 4 lemons

4 to 6 cups sugar*

Sour cream

Chopped fresh dill

6 When the borscht is quite warm, stir in the tomato paste and reserved meat. Continue to heat, and when the borscht is just below the boiling point, season it carefully with the lemon juice, salt, and sugar to taste, stirring and tasting all the while. Discard the bay leaf.

7 Serve hot, with sour cream and fresh dill.

This borscht lasts quite a while in the refrigerator and freezes well.

YIELD: 12 servings

*NOTE: In order to maintain the authenticity of this recipe, for which Lubo was renowned, the amount of sugar has been kept at 4 to 6 cups. However, the Festival's tester Alan Stein found that about 2 tablespoons were more to his taste. Alan commented that "this is a great recipe to cook all day on the back burner while keeping busy around the house on the weekend."

— *Thomas Wolf*

Strings

Gillian Ansell, *viola*
Julie Baumgartel, *violin,*
and James Mason, *oboe*
Martin Beaver, *violin*
Christiaan Bor, *violin*
Robin Lynn Braun, *violin*
Denis Brott, *cello*
Graham Campbell, *guitar*
Peter Carter, *violin*

Mark Childs, *viola*
Vicky Dvorak, *violin*
Amanda Forsyth, *cello*
Renée-Paule Gauthier, *violin*
Erica Goodman, *harp*
Moshe Hammer, *violin*
David Harding, *viola*
Patrick Jordan, *viola*
Anna Luhowy, *violin*
Annalee Patipatanakoon, *violin*
Helene Pohl, *violin*

Bruno Schrecker, *cello*
Jeffrey Stokes, *double bass*
Tsuyoshi Tsutsumi, *cello*
Christine Vlajk, *viola*
Dorothea Vogel, *viola*
Jasper Wood, *violin*
Simon Wynberg, *guitar*
Pinchas Zukerman, *violin*

GILLIAN ANSELL
Viola

Gillian Ansell is the viola player with the New Zealand String Quartet. Acclaimed for its powerful communication, dramatic energy, and beauty of sound, the New Zealand String Quartet performs more than 60 concerts each year in New Zealand and abroad. When not practising or performing, Gillian can be found growing vegetables, reading, going to movies, giving dinner parties, playing games with friends, hiking, walking, swimming in lakes, renovating houses, and having a pretty garden—but all on a strictly amateur basis.

Pasta al Limone

I got this recipe from an Italian chef on a radio program, and find it quite fabulous. The zesty freshness of lemons cutting through the richness of the cheeses creates a superb and unusual flavour explosion.

1 In a large pot of boiling salted water, cook the pasta until al dente.

2 In a large warmed bowl, whisk together the olive oil, lemon zest and juice, garlic, and chili flakes. Stir in the grated cheeses.

3 Drain the pasta and combine it with the dressing. Stir in the basil, and serve immediately with a green salad.

YIELD: 8 to 10 servings

— *Gillian Ansell*

1 pound penne or spiral pasta

⅔ cup olive oil

Zest and juice of 3 or 4 lemons

2 cloves garlic, minced (optional)

Dried chili flakes to taste

4 ounces grated Parmigiano-Reggiano cheese

4 ounces grated Grana Padano cheese

4 ounces grated Pecorino cheese

A handful of chopped fresh basil

Peruvian Chicken

An extremely easy, yet delicious and very nutritious dish, this also freezes well. The flavours all meld beautifully. This is comfort food on a cold night.

1 In a large skillet or saucepan, heat the oil over medium heat. Fry the onions, garlic, and tomato until the onions are wilted. Stir in the cilantro, lentils, and chicken stock.

2 When the lentils are nearly cooked, add the chicken, and heat for a few minutes. Be careful not to overcook. Serve over rice.

YIELD: 2 to 4 servings

VARIATIONS: You can turn this into a vegetarian dish by adding any vegetables of your choice and leaving out the chicken. I usually add carrots and something green, like Swiss chard or spinach, too. If you don't have a tomato, you could add tomato paste instead.

— *Gillian Ansell*

3 tablespoons olive oil

2 large onions, chopped

5 cloves garlic, finely chopped

1 large tomato, chopped

2 bunches cilantro, chopped

½ cup dried brown lentils (or 1 can brown lentils, drained and rinsed)

1 to 2 cups low-sodium chicken stock

2 skinless, boneless chicken breasts, cooked and chopped

Salt and pepper to taste

Sweet Green Thai Curry

This is my version of a recipe I discovered in a newspaper about 10 years ago and have since made countless times. I am a fan of many Asian flavours, and this curry tastes simply wonderful to me. Yet it can be made in the twinkling of an eye. I make small adaptations every time I make it and it always turns out fine. I add sliced carrots, or lightly fried onions, or strips of red and green pepper, or whatever other vegetables I have on hand. If I'm extremely pressed for time, the only vegetable might be a packet of frozen spinach. That works fine too!

1   Heat the oil in a large saucepan over medium-high heat. Add the curry paste, chili, and lime leaves and stir-fry for about 2 minutes. Stir in the coconut milk, fish sauce, and sugar. Bring to a boil.

2   Add the zucchini, basil, and other vegetables of your choice and cook until they are tender. Add the chicken and eggplant. Turn down the heat and simmer, stirring occasionally, until the chicken is cooked through. Be careful not to overcook the vegetables and chicken. Season with salt, and serve with rice.

YIELD: 4 servings

— *Gillian Ansell*

2 tablespoons vegetable oil

3 to 5 teaspoons green curry paste to taste

Minced fresh hot chili to taste

4 kaffir lime leaves*

3 cups coconut milk

1 tablespoon fish sauce

2 teaspoons brown sugar, or to taste

1 zucchini, sliced

1 tablespoon chopped fresh basil or mint

1 pound chicken cut in bite-sized pieces

1 small eggplant, cubed

Salt to taste

*Look for kaffir lime leaves in Asian grocery stores. You can use fresh or dried. A packet of dried leaves lasts for ages. Our recipe tester could not find kaffir lime leaves in Parry Sound, and so she substituted the grated zest of 1 lime.

Linda's Fabulous Roasted Squash Soup

JULIE BAUMGARTEL, *Violin*
JAMES MASON, *Oboe*

Husband-and-wife team Julie Baumgartel and James Mason are Founding Artistic Directors of the Grand River Baroque Festival. Violinist Julie Baumgartel has been featured in numerous CBC Radio broadcasts, was a member of Modern Quartet, and is the founder of the Festival Within a Festival chamber music concert series at the Elora Festival. James Mason is highly regarded as one of Canada's most prominent oboists. He is principal oboe of the Kitchener-Waterloo Symphony and Canadian Chamber Ensemble. He teaches at Wilfrid Laurier University, where he has the largest oboe class in Canada.

We got this recipe from our friend Linda. It's an amazing squash soup that helps us get through the winter. It's so easy, especially if you go to the Kitchener market, where they sell the acorn squashes already skinned and chopped up. You can also use parsnips.

1 Preheat the oven to 450°F.

2 In a cast-iron pan, heat the oil over medium heat. Add the squash, thyme, garlic, and chili flakes. Cook, stirring, for 10 minutes. Transfer the pan to the oven and roast for 15 minutes, stirring occasionally. (If you don't have a cast iron pan, the squash mixture can be roasted in a cake pan for 15 minutes.)

3 Remove the squash from the oven and combine it with the chicken stock. Purée the squash mixture in a blender, in batches if necessary. Reheat gently.

4 Serve with grated Parmesan cheese, if desired.

YIELD: 4 to 6 servings

— *Julie Baumgartel and James Mason*

2 tablespoons vegetable oil

1 (2-pound) butternut or acorn squash, peeled and cut into 1-inch cubes (4 to 5 cups)

½ teaspoon dried thyme

3 to 5 cloves garlic, minced

Dried chili flakes to taste

4 cups chicken stock (not from a cube)

Salt and pepper to taste

Grated Parmesan cheese, for garnish

Bourdelots (Baked Apple Buns)

MARTIN BEAVER
Violin

Martin Beaver is one of Canada's most active musicians for solo, orchestral, and chamber performances. Martin is known for a style synonymous with sensitivity, impeccable intonation, and intensity. He is currently first violin with the Tokyo String Quartet, which has captivated audiences and critics alike. The quartet performs on the Paganini Quartet, a group of renowned Stradivarius instruments named for the legendary virtuoso who acquired and played them during the nineteenth century. The instruments are on loan from the Nippon Music Foundation.

My mother picked up this recipe during her five years in Normandy (before I was even born), and it is one of my very favourite desserts. I will warn you that it is not necessarily a low-cal option!

1 Preheat the oven to 350°F. Lightly grease a baking dish large enough to comfortably fit the apples.

2 For the dough, mix the flour, sugar, and salt in a medium bowl. Using a pastry blender, cut the butter into the dry ingredients until crumbly. Gradually add the egg yolk, stirring with a fork. Add water, a little at a time, enough to bind the mixture so that the dough becomes elastic. Divide into 4 pieces, shape each piece into a ball, and set aside, covered with a cloth.

3 For the bourdelots, in a small bowl mash together the butter, 1 tablespoon sugar, and 1 teaspoon cinnamon.

4 Using a small melon baller, scoop out the core of each apple, stopping about ½ inch from the bottom. Peel the apples. Coat them with the remainder of the sugar and cinnamon mixed together. Fill the centres with the butter mixture.

5 Roll out each piece of the dough ⅛ inch thick and large enough to enclose 1 apple. Wrap each apple and transfer to the baking dish. Brush with the beaten egg.

6 Bake for 30 minutes or until lightly browned. Poke a hole in the top of each bourdelot and pour in some of the heavy cream. Serve immediately.

YIELD: 4 servings

— *Martin Beaver*

DOUGH:

1⅓ cups all-purpose flour

¼ cup sugar

A pinch of salt

½ cup unsalted butter

1 egg yolk

Water

BOURDELOTS:

3½ tablespoons unsalted butter, softened

2 tablespoons sugar

2 teaspoons cinnamon

4 McIntosh or Golden Delicious apples

1 egg, lightly beaten

1 cup heavy cream

J. HENRY FAIR

Pasta with Salmon

CHRISTIAAN BOR
Violin

Christiaan Bor made his debut with the Concertgebouw Orchestra of Amsterdam when he was 16 and has since performed as soloist with orchestras, in recitals, and in chamber music throughout Europe, Russia, the Middle East, Asia, Japan, China, Australia, New Zealand, South America, Canada, and the United States. Born in Amsterdam, he began playing the violin at the age of five as a student of his father, Jan Bor. Christiaan Bor is the founder and music director of the Amsterdam Chamber Music Society.

This dish goes well with your best bottle of white wine.

1. In a large pot of boiling salted water, cook the pasta until al dente.

2. Meanwhile, in a large skillet over medium heat, fry the garlic in the olive oil until lightly golden. Reduce the heat to low. Add the tomatoes and cook, stirring occasionally, for a few minutes. Season with salt and pepper.

3. Add the salmon and continue to simmer until the liquid has evaporated. Stir in the crème fraîche and the dill.

4. Drain the pasta, toss it with the sauce, and serve sprinkled with the Parmesan cheese.

YIELD: 4 servings

— *Christiaan Bor*

10 ounces pasta of your choice

1 clove garlic, minced

1 tablespoon extra virgin olive oil

4 tomatoes, peeled and crushed

Salt and freshly ground pepper to taste

½ pound salmon fillet, cut into small pieces

1 cup crème fraîche or sour cream

1 tablespoon finely chopped fresh dill

Freshly grated Parmesan cheese

Toffee Almond Sweets

ROBIN LYNN BRAUN
Violin

Canadian violinist Robin Lynn Braun began her musical studies at the age of five at the Suzuki String School and was appointed Concertmaster of the Kitchener-Waterloo Youth Orchestra at the age of fifteen. Robin completed an honours bachelor of music degree at Wilfrid Laurier University and a master's of music at Indiana University. She performs master violin classes around the world for violin protégés. Robin Lynn Braun is a member of the Vancouver Symphony.

1 Preheat the oven to 325°F. Butter a 13 by 9-inch cake pan.

2 For the base, in a medium bowl, combine the flour, oats, brown sugar, and baking soda. Blend in the butter until crumbly. Press the mixture into the cake pan.

3 Bake for 10 minutes. Remove the pan from the oven. Increase the oven temperature to 350°F.

4 For the filling, in a heavy saucepan, combine the corn syrup, brown sugar, evaporated milk, and butter. Stir the mixture over medium heat until it boils. Remove from the heat and stir in the almonds and vanilla. Pour the mixture over the crust, spreading evenly.

5 Bake for 15 to 20 minutes, or until golden. Cut into 2-inch-square bars while still warm. Cool on a rack. The bars keep in the pan, covered and refrigerated, for 1 week.

YIELD: 24 squares

— *Robin Lynn Braun*

BASE:

1 cup all-purpose flour

1 cup large-flake rolled oats

1 cup packed brown sugar

1 teaspoon baking soda

½ cup unsalted butter

FILLING:

½ cup corn syrup

⅓ cup packed brown sugar

¼ cup evaporated milk

¼ cup unsalted butter

1½ cups sliced almonds

1½ teaspoons vanilla

Blueberry Buttermilk Tart

DENIS BROTT
Cello

Cellist Denis Brott is recognized on the international stage as one of Canada's finest and most distinguished performing artists. Denis is chair of the Chamber Music Department and professor of cello and chamber music at the Conservatoire de musique de Montréal as well as founder and Artistic Director of the Montreal Chamber Music Festival. He played a pivotal role in the creation of the Instrument Bank of the Canada Council for the Arts, which gave him a magnificent 1706 David Tecchler cello for his lifetime use.

1 For the crust, in a bowl stir together the flour and sugar. Add the butter and cut in with a pastry blender or two knives, until the mixture resembles coarse meal. Add the yolk mixture and toss until the liquid is incorporated and the dough forms a ball. Shape the dough into a disc, dust it with flour, and chill it, or, wrapped in plastic wrap, for 1 hour.

2 On a floured surface, roll out the dough ⅛ inch thick. Fit it into a 10-inch tart pan with a removable bottom. Trim the edges. Chill the shell for at least 30 minutes, or, wrapped in plastic, overnight.

3 Preheat the oven to 350°F.

4 Line the shell with foil, fill the foil with rice or dried beans, and bake the shell in the middle of the oven for 25 minutes. Remove the foil and rice carefully. Bake the shell for 5 to 10 minutes longer, or until it is pale golden. Let it cool in the pan on a rack.

5 For the filling, in a blender or food processor, mix the buttermilk, sugar, butter, flour, lemon zest, lemon juice, vanilla, and egg yolks until smooth.

6 Spread the blueberries evenly over the bottom of the tart shell, and pour the buttermilk mixture over them. Bake in the middle of the oven for 30 to 35 minutes, or until the filling is just set.

7 Let the tart cool completely. Serve it at room temperature or chilled, with ice cream.

YIELD: 10 to 12 servings

— *Denis Brott*

CRUST:

1⅓ cups all-purpose flour

¼ cup sugar

¼ pound unsalted butter, cut into bits (½ cup)

1 large egg yolk, beaten with 2 tablespoons ice water

FILLING:

1 cup buttermilk

½ cup sugar

¼ cup unsalted butter, melted and cooled

2 tablespoons all-purpose flour

1 tablespoon freshly grated lemon zest

1 tablespoon fresh lemon juice

1 teaspoon vanilla

3 large egg yolks

2 cups fresh blueberries

Mulligatawny Soup

1   In a large skillet over medium-high heat, melt the butter until the foam subsides. Lightly sauté the onion, carrots, and celery until the onion is translucent. Stir in the flour and curry powder, and cook, stirring frequently, for 3 minutes.

2   Stir in the chicken stock, reduce the heat, and simmer for 30 minutes.

3   Stir in the chicken, cooked rice, apple, thyme, salt, and pepper. Simmer for 15 minutes longer.

YIELD: 4 servings

— Denis Brott

¼ cup butter or olive oil

1 large onion, chopped

2 large carrots, chopped

2 stalks celery, chopped

1½ tablespoons all-purpose flour

2 teaspoons curry powder

4 cups chicken stock

1 cup chopped cooked chicken

¾ cup cooked rice

1 tart apple, chopped

⅛ teaspoon dried thyme

Salt and pepper to taste

English Pancakes

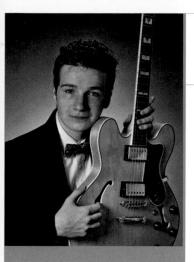

GRAHAM CAMPBELL
Jazz guitar

Graham Campbell began his music studies on piano at the age of five and later took guitar and trumpet lessons. When he was twelve, he became entranced with the jazz playing of pianist Gene DiNovi, and from that time on jazz became his passion. During Graham's senior year in high school he took undergraduate and graduate courses in the jazz program at Indiana University. His composition "Tune for Andy" was recorded by his father, Jim, Gene DiNovi, and bassist Dave Young. He is studying jazz at Humber College in Toronto.

This is the one recipe that I have learned from my mother. Because I love these pancakes so much, I decided it was much easier to learn how to make them myself, rather than asking her to make them for me. They are the pancakes traditionally eaten in England on Shrove Tuesday, and used for pancake races around the country on that day.

1. Mix the flour and salt in a bowl. Make a well in the flour, and plop in the egg. (Take the egg out of its shell first!) Stir the egg with a fork, gradually drawing in the flour. Slowly add the milk. Mix well with a whisk. Add the water and mix again.

2. Melt the shortening in an 8-inch skillet or griddle over high heat. When the pan is smoking hot, add enough batter to cover the bottom of the pan, making a *thin* pancake resembling a crêpe.

3. When the underside is golden, flip the pancake. Cook for a few minutes more. The surface of the pancake should look a bit like lace.

4. Transfer the pancake to a plate and keep warm. Continue to cook pancakes, adding additional shortening to the pan as needed. Sprinkle the pancakes with sugar and lemon juice. Roll up.

YIELD: 5 thin pancakes, or 1 serving

SUGGESTION: For a hungry family, have two frying pans going at once. Cook the first pancake; flip it into the second pan; then start another pancake in the first pan.

— *Graham Campbell*

Heaping ¼ cup all-purpose flour

¼ teaspoon salt

1 large egg

½ cup milk

½ cup water

1 tablespoon shortening

Sugar and lemon juice to taste

Maggie Haxby's Italian Trifle

PETER CARTER
Violin

Peter Carter is regarded as one of the most influential and experienced chamber musicians in the U.K. He was leader of the Allegri String Quartet from 1976 to his retirement in 2005, confirming its reputation both nationally and internationally as one of the most respected and widely recorded chamber groups. Peter was born in Durban, South Africa; his is the fourth generation of his family to have a professional musician.

Maggie Haxby is a great friend who spends a lot of time in Italy. This is an easy and delicious dessert that always draws "oohs" and "aahs" from guests, as it is quite rich. Make it a day in advance if you can as, like all trifles, this gives it time to draw the juices out. It's still good, but drier, if you only have time to make it the same day. It's a three-layer "pud"—the fruit at the bottom, then the crushed biscuits, then a syllabub rather than a custard on the top.

1 In a bowl, whisk together the cream, brandy, sherry, sugar, lemon zest and juice until thick but light.

2 Crush the amaretti (in a plastic bag and using a rolling pin) until they are like coarse bread crumbs.

3 Clean and dry the raspberries.

4 Put the raspberries in the bottom of a glass serving bowl. Scatter the crushed biscuits over them. Spread the syllabub over all. Sprinkle with the almonds (if desired).

YIELD: 6 to 8 servings

— *Peter Carter*

1¼ cups heavy cream

2 tablespoons brandy

A small wine glass of sweet sherry or (even better) Madeira

2 tablespoons granulated sugar

Zest and juice of 1 lemon

1 pound amaretti biscuits (the crunchy macaroon type, not the soft "morbidi" type)

4 cups raspberries (strawberries work well but are not as flavoursome when soft)

2 tablespoons toasted slivered almonds

Markey's Pickles

MARK CHILDS
Viola

Well-known to Canadian audiences as solo violist of the Hamilton Philharmonic from 1976 until 1988, Mark Childs was also Artist-in-Residence at McMaster University from 1978 to 1989. Now a resident of Toronto, Mark is also violist with the Amati Quartet and is in great demand as a teacher and coach. With Trio Lyra, he has thrilled and enticed concertgoers since 1978 with a wide variety of music for the combination of flute, viola, and harp.

My pickles are legendary among my friends and family. These are the kind you used to get from a barrel in the delis on the East Side of New York. When I had my own vegetable garden, I used to plant pickling cukes all along the chain-link fence bordering the garden and dill plants all around the area. In the height of the season, I could pick three to four quarts a day and jar them immediately. Pickles made this way are amazing.

P.S. Having lived in downtown Toronto for the past 18 years, I haven't been able to make these for decades. If anyone has success with this recipe, PLEASE send me some!

1 Sterilize 3 or 4 one-quart canning jars and their lids.

2 Dissolve the salt in the water and bring to a boil to make a brine. Cool.

3 Rinse the cukes thoroughly in cold water. Put the cukes in the jars, packing tightly. Stuff into the available space in each jar 1 enormous clove of garlic (or 2 or 3 smaller ones), 2 to 4 sprigs dill, and ½ tablespoon pickling spice. Fill the jars to the brim with the brine.

4 Oil the rim of each jar and tighten the lid as much as possible. Leave the jars in the basement or other cool, dark place for 14 days to ferment. (I strongly suggest putting the jars in a bucket or tub in case any of them explodes while fermenting!) The pickles keep indefinitely in the refrigerator.

YIELD: 3 or 4 quarts

— *Mark Childs*

⅓ cup kosher salt

7 cups water

3 or 4 quarts pickling cucumbers

4 enormous cloves garlic (or 8 to 12 smaller ones), crushed

8 to 16 sprigs fresh dill

2 tablespoons pickling spice

A little vegetable oil

GADI HOZ

Pernik (Spice Loaf)

VICKY DVORAK
Violin

Born in Toronto, Vicky Dvorak completed a music-performance degree in violin at the University of Toronto under Lorand Fenyves. She continued her studies at McGill University in Montreal with Mauricio Fuks. Vicky now lives in Kitchener, where she has just completed her eleventh season as a violinist with the Kitchener-Waterloo Symphony.

Here is a recipe that has been passed down from my maternal grandmother, Brigita Stalmach, who was an opera singer in Prague. "Pernik" is a spice loaf from Czechoslovakia. We especially liked to take it with us as a sweet treat on trips when we were kids because it keeps very well and actually increases in flavour and moistness as it ages.

1. Preheat the oven to 325°F. Grease and flour a 12-cup Bundt pan or 2 loaf pans.

2. Melt the honey in the hot water. Stir in the sugar until dissolved. Set aside to cool.

3. Beat the eggs until thick and lemon-coloured, and stir them into the cooled honey mixture.

4. Sift the flour, baking powder, cinnamon, cloves, allspice, anise, and baking soda into a large bowl. Stir in the nuts and lemon zest.

5. Pour the honey mixture into the flour mixture, and stir only until the batter is evenly moistened. Pour the batter into the cake pan.

6. Bake for 1 hour, or until a toothpick inserted in the centre comes out clean. Cool and decorate, if you wish, with lemon icing and blanched almonds. Wrap the cake well and store it in a cool place.

YIELD: 1 Bundt cake or 2 loaves

— *Vicky Dvorak*

2 cups honey (or 1 cup honey and 1 cup corn syrup)

1 cup hot water

1 cup sugar

2 large eggs

4 cups all-purpose flour

2 teaspoons baking powder

1 teaspoon cinnamon

½ teaspoon ground cloves

½ teaspoon ground allspice

½ teaspoon ground anise seed

¼ teaspoon baking soda

½ cup coarsely chopped almonds and/or hazelnuts

1½ teaspoons lemon zest

AMANDA FORSYTH
Cello

Canadian Juno award–winner Amanda Forsyth is considered one of North America's most dynamic cellists. Born in South Africa, she came to Canada as a child and began playing the cello at age three. By the age of 24, she had performed two seasons with the Toronto Symphony and was appointed principal cellist of the Calgary Philharmonic. In 1999, Amanda was appointed principal cellist with the National Arts Centre Orchestra, with which she also appears regularly as a soloist and in chamber ensembles.

Salmon Tartare

I love fish of all kinds and eat salmon or trout almost every day. It's really good for you, and gives you energy and those all-important omega 3 oils. Not to mention helping with those juicy slides we all need for fabulous music. Actually, I don't really spend much time cooking, but I enjoy chopping and combining! I make good spicy dips and enjoy doing salmon tartare for special occasions. This recipe is for two people, to be eaten with lovely chilled French Champagne. The quantities in the recipe are "guesstimates." Trust your own taste buds!

1 Skin the salmon and chop it into ¼-inch dice. Combine the salmon, green onions, olive oil, capers and their juice, soy sauce, and pepper. Stir gently to combine. Adjust the seasoning.

2 Just before serving, add lemon juice to taste.

3 Spoon the mixture into martini glasses, and garnish with chives.

YIELD: serves 2 as an appetizer, or just to have with champagne

— *Amanda Forsyth*

1 fillet of the freshest salmon, about 3 inches wide

2 green onions, finely chopped

2 tablespoons extra virgin olive oil

1 tablespoon capers, chopped, plus 1 teaspoon of the juice

1 tablespoon soy sauce

Freshly ground pepper to taste

Freshly squeezed lemon juice to taste

Chives, for garnish

Sucre à la Crème

RENÉE-PAULE GAUTHIER
Violin

Violinist Renée-Paule Gauthier was recently named one of the "best upcoming violinists of the new generation." Until January 2004, Renée-Paule was concertmaster of the New World Symphony in Miami Beach. She currently resides in Ottawa, performing with the National Arts Centre Orchestra. Outside of music, her passions are her husband and family and also yoga, running, and fitness. She recently took up painting. Her dream is to improve to the point where, one day, her artwork will be on the Festival of the Sound poster!

This French-Canadian white fudge is particularly enjoyable backstage during intermission!

1 Butter a 9-inch square pan.

2 In a medium saucepan, combine the brown sugar and the butter. Slowly melt the mixture over low heat while stirring constantly. (This recipe, you'll see, doubles as an upper body workout.) Increase the heat and bring the mixture to a boil.

3 Add the evaporated milk. Return to the boil, then reduce heat and let simmer for 5 minutes while stirring constantly.

4 Remove from the heat. Using an electric mixer, beat in the confectioners' sugar. The mixture will start to harden pretty fast.

5 Spread the fudge in the buttered pan and let set. Cut into squares.

YIELD: 48 squares

— *Renée-Paule Gauthier*

3 cups packed brown sugar

1 cup butter (½ pound)

1 (5-ounce) can evaporated milk

2 cups confectioners' sugar

Maple Butter Cheesecake with Pecans

ERICA GOODMAN
Harp

A native of Toronto, Erica Goodman is acclaimed as one of the world's outstanding solo harpists. She received her training at the Royal Conservatory of Music, the National Music Camp at Interlochen, and the Curtis Institute of Music. As Canada's foremost studio harpist, Erica has played in hundreds of radio and TV productions, commercials, and film scores. She has been a soloist at numerous international festivals and with leading orchestras and ensembles worldwide. Her love of chamber music is highlighted by her long association with Trio Lyra.

Here are two of my favourite recipes, both using maple products—a fitting Canadian way to celebrate a music festival that has become a Canadian institution.

1. Preheat the oven to 350°F. Lightly grease the sides of a 10-inch springform pan.

2. Toast the chopped pecans in a single layer on a cookie sheet for 5 to 10 minutes. Watch closely to avoid burning. Remove from the oven and turn the temperature down to 325°F.

3. In a medium bowl, combine the pecans, graham cracker crumbs, butter, and maple syrup. Press the mixture into the bottom of the pan in an even layer. Bake for 10 minutes, or until lightly browned.

4. Cut the cream cheese into chunks. In a food processor or with an electric mixer, beat the cheese until smooth. Add the maple butter, flour, eggs, vanilla, and salt. Process the mixture until smooth. Pour it over the crust.

5. Bake for 35 to 40 minutes, or until the outer edge of the filling is firm but the centre is still soft.

6. Remove the cheesecake from the oven, and immediately run a table knife around the inside of the pan. This will prevent the filling from cracking as it cools. Cool on a rack to room temperature, then chill in the refrigerator.

7. Remove the sides from the pan, and transfer the cake to a serving plate. Just before serving, spread the 2 tablespoons maple syrup over the cake and arrange the pecan halves around the edge.

YIELD: 16 slim pieces

— *Erica Goodman*

CRUST:

½ cup chopped pecans

1¼ cups graham cracker or shortbread crumbs

3 tablespoons butter, melted

2 tablespoons maple syrup

FILLING:

3 (8-ounce/250 gram) packages cream cheese

¾ cup maple butter or real maple syrup

2 tablespoons all-purpose flour

3 eggs

2 teaspoons vanilla

A pinch of salt

TOPPING:

2 tablespoons maple syrup

16 toasted pecan halves

GADI HOZ

Maple Teriyaki Salmon

1 In a nonreactive baking dish, combine the maple syrup, wine, soy sauce, onion, pepper, and sesame seeds (if using). Add the salmon steaks and splash the sauce over the salmon. Marinate, covered and refrigerated, for up to 3 hours.

2 Broil or barbecue the salmon steaks for 3 to 5 minutes per side, basting with the marinade.

YIELD: 4 servings

— *Erica Goodman*

⅓ cup maple syrup

⅓ cup dry white wine or sherry

3 tablespoons soy sauce

1 small onion, minced

Freshly ground black pepper to taste

Sesame seeds to taste (optional)

4 salmon steaks, each 1 inch thick

MOSHE HAMMER
Violin

Admired for his artistic style, unique interpretations, and vibrant tone, violinist Moshe Hammer remains Canada's most sought-after violinist for solo, concerto, and chamber appearances. His career has taken him across North America, Israel, and Western Europe, including Spain, Belgium, Sweden, Holland, Germany, Portugal, Scotland, and Wigmore Hall in London. Hungarian-born, Moshe was raised in Israel, first cultivated his sound under the guidance of Ilona Feher, and received scholarships to study in the U.S. with Jascha Heifetz.

Sweet Potato Fries

As much as I love french fries, I love these even more!

1   Preheat the oven to 425°F.

2   Cut the sweet potatoes french fry style. Place them in a mixing bowl. Add the oil, tamari, salt, and pepper. Toss until the potatoes are well coated.

3   Spread on a baking sheet and bake for 5 to 7 minutes, until golden brown. Turn the fries over and bake for another 5 to 7 minutes, until golden brown and crisp.

4   Serve with eggs and toast for a hearty breakfast.

YIELD: 4 servings

— *Moshe Hammer*

2 large sweet potatoes

2 tablespoons olive oil

2 tablespoons tamari soy sauce

½ teaspoon salt

3 pinches of pepper

Quick Red Pesto

DAVID HARDING
Viola

A two-time prize winner at the Lionel Tertis International Viola Competition, David Harding is one of this generation's most sought-after violists. As a soloist and chamber musician, he has performed in concerts and festivals throughout the world. He is a member of two Canadian chamber ensembles, Triskelion and the Toronto String Quartet. A native of Toronto, he is a graduate of the Juilliard School and today is a professor of viola at the University of British Columbia. He plays a viola made by Pietro Antonio della Costa circa 1750.

This quick pesto makes a great hostess gift. A double recipe fills a 1-cup jar.

I   Place all the ingredients in a food processor and purée until smooth.

2   The pesto can be stored in a jar in the fridge for up to a month. If doing so, cover the pesto with a thin film of olive oil.

3   The pesto may be tossed into pasta or spread on bread, or used as an antipasto dip.

YIELD: ½ cup

— *David Harding*

About 20 salt-cured olives (such as Gaeta, Nyons, or Kalamata), pitted

10 sun-dried tomatoes in oil

1 clove garlic, minced

1 tablespoon minced fresh rosemary

2 teaspoons minced fresh thyme

½ teaspoon dried chili flakes, or to taste

6 tablespoons extra virgin olive oil

PATRICK JORDAN
Viola

Patrick Jordan, a native of Texas, is a member of Tafelmusik Baroque Orchestra. He is in demand across North America as a chamber and orchestral musician, and has been a member of the Boston Early Music Festival since 1997. Patrick is also violist and Artistic Administrator of the Gallery Players of Niagara, and is a member of Eybler Quartet. He is currently on the faculty of the Royal Conservatory of Music. He has included four recipes, one for each season: Spinach Farfalle for spring, Soupe au Pistou for summer, Warm Cabbage Salad for fall, and Pork Chops with Sage for winter.

Spinach Farfalle

The combination of sheep's milk cheese with cream and an acidic leafy green like spinach is very hard to beat. You could easily substitute soft goat cheese for the Crotonese for a gentler sauce, or use Swiss chard in place of the spinach. Of course if you are not up to making pasta from scratch—even though it is surprisingly easy—you can use 1 pound of dried farfalle.

1. Steam the spinach in a heavy saucepan over medium heat, covered, with no water added, just until wilted, about 3 minutes. Drain in a colander, pressing out the liquid. Blot the excess moisture with paper towels. Cool.

2. In a food processor, pulse together the cooled spinach and the parsley until chopped. Add the flour and pulse for a few seconds to blend. Add the eggs and pulse again, scraping down the sides of the bowl as needed. Process, adding more flour 1 tablespoon at a time if necessary, until the mixture resembles coarse meal or raw couscous (rather than dough). You should be able to pinch a lump and have it hold together but not be dough-like or sticky.

3. Divide the mixture in half, and place each half on a sheet of plastic wrap. Use the wrap to gather the mixture into a ball and press into a rectangle about ⅓ to ¼ inch thick. Wrap the dough tightly and let rest for at least 30 minutes at room temperature. (This rest is essential to allow the gluten in the flour to relax, otherwise it will not be workable when you try to roll it out.)

4. Set the rollers of a pasta machine at the largest (#1) setting. Dust 2 cookie sheets well with cornmeal, for spreading out the cut pasta to dry. (Cornmeal works better than flour to prevent pasta from sticking; it falls off during the cooking.)

(continued on next page)

PASTA (recipe provided by Leslie Crawford):

1 (6-ounce/170 gram) bag fresh spinach, washed and tough stems removed

1 bunch fresh flat-leaf parsley, washed and well dried

1⅓ cups all-purpose flour, plus more as needed

2 large eggs

Cornmeal (for dusting the cookie sheets)

SAUCE:

¼ cup unsalted butter

1 clove garlic, minced

1 (6-ounce/170 gram) bag fresh spinach, washed, tough stems removed, and sliced into 1 inch strips

1½ cups heavy cream

7 ounces Crotonese (hard sheep's milk cheese), finely grated (or Parmigiano-Reggiano or Romano)

5 Unwrap one piece of dough and cut it in half. Rewrap the second half. If the dough feels at all sticky, dust it with flour. Pass it through the rollers of the pasta maker. If the pasta breaks apart somewhat, rotate the pasta so that it goes through the rollers at a different angle. Continue to pass it through the rollers, still at the same setting, three or four more times until it holds its shape. Continue passing through the rollers on settings 2, 3, 4, 5, and 6 until you have a long scarf-like piece that may be easier to handle if you cut it in half.

6 Cut the dough crosswise into 2-inch-wide strips with a fluted pastry cutter. Cut each strip into ½-inch-wide pieces. Gather each piece at the centre, pinching well to form a bowtie. Spread the farfalle on the cookie sheets, making sure they are not touching each other, and dust them well with cornmeal. Continue to roll and cut the remaining pieces of dough in the same way. (Or you can use the cutting rollers of the pasta maker to make fettuccine or linguine or whatever shapes your pasta maker allows.)

7 Make the sauce while the pasta dries slightly. It is ready to be cooked when it is somewhat drier but still flexible. (Or place it in plastic bags and refrigerate or freeze it.)
Warning: This pasta contains raw egg and so must be refrigerated if it's not to be used soon.

8 Bring a large pot of water to a boil for the pasta.

9 In a heavy saucepan over low heat, melt the butter. Add the garlic and cook, covered, for 2 to 4 minutes until the garlic is softened but not brown. Add the spinach with its clinging water, and turn the heat up to medium. Cover and cook, stirring occasionally, for 5 minutes or until the spinach is wilted.

10 Add the cream and increase the heat to medium-high. Cook until the cream is reduced by half.

11 Add salt to the boiling water and cook the pasta until just al dente, 3 to 5 minutes.

12 Turn the heat under the sauce down to low, and stir in half the cheese, stirring constantly until it is melted. Repeat with the other half of the cheese.

13 Stir in the drained pasta and season with salt and pepper. Serve immediately, sprinkled with the pine nuts.

YIELD: 4 to 6 servings

— *Patrick Jordan*

Salt and pepper to taste

1 handful pine nuts, toasted

Soupe au Pistou

This soup is commonly served in the summertime in Provence, and it was while playing at the summer music and theatre festival in Aix-en-Provence that I first tasted it. My first bowl was at a restaurant called La Félibre. I remember sitting outside as the evening arrived. It was probably 8:30, and we were the first group of the evening (which was rewarded by a bottle, gratis, of Provençal rosé wine). When the soup arrived, I was overcome by the incredibly unctuous garlic and basil aromas that were caressing and tweaking my face. The preparation is very simple, very flexible, and very economical when everything is in season. Rosé is a great wine match.

1   In a pot of boiling salted water, cook the pasta until al dente. Drain, rinse under cold water, and set aside.

2   In a large saucepan, cover the potatoes with the quart of water. Add salt and bring to a boil. Lower the heat and simmer for 5 minutes. Add the romano beans. Return the soup to a boil, then reduce heat again and simmer for 5 minutes. Continue in this manner with the green beans, zucchini, and tomatoes, the goal being that all the vegetables are done at about the same time.

3   In the meantime, make the pistou, either in a mortar and pestle or a food processor. Put the garlic in first and sprinkle with the salt. Let sit for a few minutes. Add the basil, a handful at a time, pounding (or pulsing) to achieve a smooth paste. Grind in the pepper to taste. Add the olive oil, 2 tablespoons at a time, stirring and pounding (or pulsing) until the mixture is smooth, unctuous, and quite sharp to the taste.

4   Add the reserved pasta to the soup and simmer until the pasta is heated through. (If the pasta sits in the soup too long, it begins to swell up and takes over the soup in a cartoonish way). Serve the soup in heated bowls, passing the pistou and cheese to be added to each diner's taste.

YIELD: serves 4 as a starter, or 2 as a substantial meal with bread

— *Patrick Jordan*

SOUP:

1 handful small pasta

2 medium potatoes, peeled and cut in ½-inch dice

1 quart water (plus a little more if needed)

2 or 3 teaspoons salt

1 big handful fresh or frozen romano beans

1 handful green beans, cut in 1-inch lengths

2 small (or 1 medium) zucchini, quartered lengthwise and cut into ½-inch chunks

2 medium tomatoes (or 4 plum tomatoes), peeled, seeded, and diced

4 to 6 ounces Emmental, Gruyère, or Parmesan cheese, grated

PISTOU:

4 cloves garlic, minced

1½ teaspoons salt

2 cups tightly packed fresh basil

Abundant ground black pepper

At least ½ cup extra virgin olive oil

Steamed Savoy Cabbage (Warm Cabbage Salad)

One of the benefits of travelling as a musician is the opportunity to taste new foods in their native locale. This warm cabbage salad is an example of how we have to remain open-minded about where a new dish might come from: I was inspired to make this by something similar I was served on a Lufthansa flight over the Atlantic! The combination of cream and mustard both calms down and perks up the flavour of the cabbage. Let's hear it for (the very occasional example of) airplane food!

1 Steam the cabbage for 10 minutes, or until it is as tender as you like.

2 In a large bowl, whisk together the cream, mustard, garlic, salt, and pepper. Add the hot cabbage and toss well. Serve hot, warm, or at room temperature.

YIELD: 6 servings as a side dish

— *Patrick Jordan*

½ large head Savoy cabbage, cut crosswise into ½-inch slices

⅓ cup heavy cream

3 tablespoons strong Dijon mustard

1 clove garlic, minced

2 teaspoons salt

Pepper to taste

Pork Chops with Sage

This recipe is adapted from one in La Véritable Cuisine Provençale et Niçoise *by Jean-Noël Escudier. He suggests these chops be grilled and served without sauce, accompanied by broiled stuffed tomatoes. I found myself making this dish once without a grill, and so sautéed the chops instead; I just couldn't bear to leave all that tasty stuff behind in the pan . . .*

1   Score the chops lightly in a cross-hatch pattern. Rub most of the sage mixture in very well. Set aside remaining sage mixture.

2   In a skillet over medium-high heat, heat enough olive oil to just coat the bottom of the pan. When the oil is very hot but not smoking, brown the chops well on both sides until no longer pink inside. Do not overcook. Remove the chops from the pan and keep warm.

3   Add the garlic to the pan and stir twice. Add the anchovies and remaining sage mixture; stir until the anchovies dissolve. Add the vermouth and deglaze the pan, stirring to scrape up any brown bits. Let the sauce reduce until syrupy.

4   Lower the heat and add 1 teaspoon of the butter while stirring. When the butter has almost melted, add another teaspoon. Continue adding butter and stirring until all the butter is used.

5   Dress the chops with the sauce and serve immediately.

— *Patrick Jordan*

Thin-cut pork loin chops (1 or 2 per person)

Mixture of 1 teaspoon rubbed sage, ½ teaspoon pepper, and ¼ teaspoon salt per chop

Olive oil

1 clove garlic per pork chop, minced

½ anchovy fillet per pork chop

Dry vermouth (enough to deglaze the pan)

1 tsp unsalted butter per pork chop

Chocolate Truffle Cake

ANNA LUHOWY
Violin

Anna Luhowy has been with the Kitchener-Waterloo Symphony for nearly 30 years. She currently holds the position of Assistant Concertmaster. A native of Winnipeg, Anna began her violin studies at the age of eight and was chosen to participate in the National Youth Orchestra of Canada in 1972. One of her proudest accomplishments has been creating and producing the infamous KWS calendars for the years 1995 and '96. In her spare time Anna enjoys fitness training and has a passion for movies.

This very easy (no baking required) cake has to be my all-time favourite dessert. Definitely a hit with chocoholics!!

1 Line the base of a 9-inch springform pan with parchment or waxed paper. Sprinkle the amaretti crumbs over the base of the pan. Set aside.

2 In the top of a double boiler, or in a bowl set over hot (not boiling) water, melt the chocolate and butter, stirring occasionally, until smooth. Stir in the amaretto. Remove from the heat and let cool at room temperature until thickened but not set, about 1 hour.

3 In a large bowl, whip the cream until it holds stiff peaks. Fold the cream into the chocolate mixture. Pour the chocolate-cream mixture into the prepared pan, spreading evenly.

4 Refrigerate, covered, for at least 4 hours or overnight, until firm.

5 To serve, invert the pan onto a serving plate and release the sides. Remove the pan bottom. Garnish with extra whipped cream, if desired.

6 The dessert can be refrigerated, covered, up to 3 days or frozen up to 2 weeks. Thaw overnight in the refrigerator.

YIELD: 12 to 16 servings

— *Anna Luhowy*

⅔ cup amaretti cookie crumbs (Ameretti can be found in an Italian grocery store or a gourmet shop)

1 pound best-quality bittersweet chocolate, chopped

¼ pound butter (½ cup)

⅓ cup amaretto

2 cups heavy cream, plus extra for garnish, if desired

Marinated Asparagus

Easy but elegant, this recipe makes a fabulous salad dressing. I would recommend serving it on the side. It's quite thick and is better drizzled on at the last moment.

1   For the vinaigrette, pulse the shallot and garlic in a food processor until finely chopped. Add the vinegar, mustard, salt, lemon juice, and pepper; process briefly to combine. With the motor running, add the olive oil in a very slow but steady stream, processing until the dressing is emulsified. Set aside.

2   Blanch the asparagus, then drain and refresh in cold water. Drain again and dry thoroughly on paper towels. Let stand at room temperature.

3   Thirty minutes before serving, arrange the asparagus attractively on a platter and drizzle with the vinaigrette. Sprinkle with toasted sesame seeds. Serve at room temperature.

YIELD: 8 servings

— *Anna Luhowy*

1 small shallot

1 clove garlic

1 tablespoon balsamic vinegar

1½ teaspoons Dijon mustard

½ teaspoon salt

Juice of ½ lemon

Freshly ground black pepper to taste

½ cup olive oil

2 pounds asparagus, ends trimmed

2 tablespoons sesame seeds, toasted

The Perfect Steak

1 Rinse the steaks and pat dry with paper towels. In a nonreactive dish or heavy plastic bag, combine the oil, soy sauce, balsamic vinegar, Worcestershire sauce, mustard, garlic, and pepper. Add the steaks, turning to coat, and marinate for 1 hour at room temperature, or up to 24 hours in refrigerator, covered. If refrigerating, bring steaks close to room temperature 30 minutes before grilling, for more even cooking.

2 Preheat the barbecue to high and brush the grids with olive oil. Place the steaks on the hot grids on one side of the barbecue and turn the heat on that side down to medium. Close the lid and grill the steaks for 2½ minutes, then rotate the steaks one-quarter turn to create a crisscross pattern. Close the lid and grill for another 2½ minutes.

3 Turn the steaks over onto the hot grids on the other side of the barbecue. Reduce the heat on this side of the barbecue to medium and close the lid. For medium doneness, grill steaks for 2½ minutes. Rotate the steaks one-quarter turn, close the lid, and grill for 2½ more minutes.

YIELD: 4 servings

— *Anna Luhowy*

4 tenderloin steaks, each 1½ inches thick

1 tablespoon olive oil

1 tablespoon soy sauce

1 tablespoon balsamic vinegar

1 tablespoon Worcestershire sauce

1 teaspoon Dijon mustard

2 or 3 cloves garlic, minced or pressed

Plenty of freshly ground black pepper

Almond Roca

ANNALEE PATIPATANAKOON
Violin

Annalee Patipatanakoon is the violinist with the Gryphon Trio. The Gryphon Trio is recognized as one of North America's premier chamber ensembles. The trio is named after the gryphon, a mythical creature that is half lion and half eagle. The gryphon is reputed to be a guardian of treasures and a symbol of the connection between psychic energy and cosmic force. Trio members Annalee Patipatanakoon, Jamie Parker, and Roman Borys all teach at the University of Toronto Faculty of Music.

It took me a few tries to perfect this recipe. The type of pot, the temperature, and how much you stir all affect the success of the candy. Of course, the more expensive the chocolate, the better it is as well! Highly recommended by the Gryphon Trio.

1 Melt the butter in a heavy saucepan over medium heat. Add the sugar, water, and corn syrup. Cook, stirring frequently, taking care not to let the mixture burn, until the sugar has dissolved.

2 Increase the heat to medium-high. Cook, stirring, until the mixture reaches 285°F on a candy thermometer (soft crack stage). The mixture should look light to medium brown in colour. Quickly stir in ½ cup of the almonds, preferably the larger pieces.

3 Immediately pour the mixture onto an ungreased baking sheet, and spread it evenly. Wait 2 to 3 minutes for the surface to become firm.

4 Melt the chocolate in a small bowl set over barely simmering water. Do not let any water or steam touch the chocolate. Alternatively, you can microwave it on medium-high, stirring every 30 seconds, until melted.

5 Pour the melted chocolate over the firm candy and spread it evenly. Sprinkle the remaining almonds over the chocolate. (To be decadent, melt twice the amount of chocolate and use twice the amount of almonds. Spread half the chocolate over the candy

(continued on next page)

1 cup salted butter

1 cup sugar

2 tablespoons water

1 teaspoon light corn syrup

1 cup finely chopped toasted almonds (leave some coarsely chopped)

1 cup (more is better!) chopped good-quality semisweet chocolate

and sprinkle with half the almonds. Flip over the candy and wait 2 or 3 minutes for the surface to become firm. Again, pour melted chocolate over the candy and spread. Sprinkle remaining almonds over the chocolate.)

6 The candy takes 1 day to set. Once hard, break the candy apart, and serve. The candy keeps several days in a covered container.

YIELD: more than one person should eat in one sitting!

— *Annalee Patipatanakoon*

Oatmeal Pancakes

HELENE POHL
Violin

Born in Ithaca, New York, to German parents, Helene Pohl spent her childhood on both sides of the Atlantic and began her musical studies at age four. At 17 she was accepted for tertiary study at the Musikhochschule Cologne. Helene joined the New Zealand String Quartet as first violinist in 1994. In 2001 she became Artistic Director, with fellow quartet member Gillian Ansell, of the Adam New Zealand Festival of Chamber Music. Helene and her husband, Rolf Gjelsten, the cellist with the New Zealand String Quartet, recently welcomed their first child.

These pancakes are my weekend-morning staple. I like to serve them to guests, too. They can be eaten either sweet—with maple syrup, fruit, jam, yogurt, whipped cream—or savoury—with cheese and avocado. They really fill you up, and keep you that way for hours. It makes sense, when it's basically oat porridge!

The thickness is part of the charm of these pancakes, but in order to get them to cook evenly, you don't want them too thick. You'll have to experiment to find what works for you.

1 In a large bowl, combine the oats, honey, and molasses. Let the mixture stand at room temperature overnight to let the oats soften.

2 Sift the flour, baking soda, and salt over the oat mixture and stir to combine. Stir in the eggs and yogurt to make a batter. Stir in a little milk or water if the batter is too thick. Stir in the nuts and raisins (if using).

3 Heat a heavy skillet or griddle over medium-high heat. Melt the butter, and turn the heat down to medium. Spoon the pancake batter onto the griddle by ¼ cupfuls. Flip the pancakes when bubbles appear on the top and the bottom is golden. The pancakes are done when both sides are golden. Keep them warm in a 200°F oven while you make the others.

4 Once the pan is seasoned after the first round of pancakes, no more oil should be needed. Because the later batches of pancakes are not greasy, they save really well, and can be heated up later for snacks.

YIELD: 4 to 6 servings

— *Helene Pohl*

1½ cups large-flake rolled oats

¼ to ½ cup honey or other sweetener

2 tablespoons molasses

1 cup whole wheat flour

1 teaspoon baking soda

A pinch of salt

2 large eggs, lightly beaten

2 cups yogurt, buttermilk, sour milk, or a combination*

Chopped nuts and raisins (optional)

2 tablespoons unsalted butter or vegetable oil

*You want something fermented for the taste, so if all you have is fresh milk, add a splash of vinegar or lemon juice to sour it

Bruno's Lamb and Lentil Casserole

BRUNO SCHRECKER
Cello

Cellist Bruno Schrecker was a member of the Allegri String Quartet for many years. Colleagues past and present speak with awe of Bruno's sense of anticipation—his ability to "include them in," musically. Voluble, passionate, energetic, he had and has a wonderful sense of humour. For example, after a concert where the quartet outnumbered the backstage admirers, he said: "You can let in the first 20!" And yet behind the jokes, there is a deep sense of responsibility, of the music being greater than the individual players.

This is a tasty dish that would be nice as part of a buffet.

1 Preheat the oven to 400°F.

2 In a small bowl, combine the lemon juice, olive oil, and garlic. Brush or rub this mixture over the lamb. Season the lamb with the oregano, salt, and pepper.

3 Place the onion and carrots in a casserole dish large enough to hold the lamb. Set the lamb on top of the onion and carrots and pour the wine around the lamb. Cover the casserole lightly with foil, place the lid on the dish, and cook for 20 minutes. Reduce the oven temperature to 300°F, and cook for 2 hours.

4 Wash the lentils and put them in a saucepan. Add enough water to cover them by ½ inch. Bring to a boil, and boil for 15 minutes. Drain (reserve the cooking liquid if you are using it instead of stock).

5 Add the lentils, tomatoes, and stock to the casserole. Cover and cook for 20 minutes.

6 Remove the lamb from the casserole dish and pull the meat from the bone. Stir the meat into the lentil mixture and return to the oven to reheat.

YIELD: 4 servings

— *Bruno Schrecker*

Juice of ½ lemon

1 tablespoon olive oil

1 clove garlic, minced

1 (4 to 5-pound) lamb shoulder roast, or lamb shanks

1 teaspoon dried oregano

Salt and black pepper to taste

1 large onion, thinly sliced

4 carrots, thickly sliced

¾ cup red wine

1 cup green lentils

1 (14-ounce/398 mL) can peeled tomatoes, drained and chopped

1 cup chicken stock (or lentil cooking water)

Crusty Baked Eggplant

JEFFREY STOKES
Double bass

Jeffrey Stokes studied double bass and musicology at the Eastman School of Music of the University of Rochester. He followed this with a PhD in musicology at the State University of New York at Buffalo. Currently he is Director of Graduate Studies in Music at the University of Western Ontario. Jeffrey is involved in both studio teaching and graduate seminars. He continues to perform and record as a chamber player and narrator-actor and with orchestras throughout Ontario and to lecture, adjudicate, and give clinics.

These rounds are crunchy on the outside and creamy on the inside. They can be served as a vegetable side dish or cut into wedges for warm hors d'oeuvres.

1   Preheat the oven to 425°F. Lightly spray a baking sheet with cooking spray.

2   Mix together the Parmesan and bread crumbs. Thinly spread the mayonnaise on both sides of the eggplant rounds. Press the rounds into the crumb mixture, generously coating both sides. Arrange them in a single layer on the baking sheet.

3   Bake for 8 to 10 minutes, until browned. Turn the rounds over and bake for about 5 minutes longer, until creamy on the inside and crunchy on the outside.

YIELD: 4 servings

— Jeffrey Stokes

½ cup grated Parmesan cheese

½ cup dry bread crumbs

Mayonnaise

1 large eggplant, peeled and sliced into rounds about ¾ inch thick

Salad with Feta and Spiced Pecans

While studying at the Eastman School of Music, I had a student job in the kitchens of the residence hall. We were presided over by a hotel-trained chef, a short Italian man named Michael Forte (appropriate enough for a music school, eh?). Over the years I worked my way up from pot washer to his assistant. This meant that on most Sundays, I and another student assistant would work with him directly to prepare the evening meal for about 450 diners.

The mass meal was itself great, much more like a good restaurant's than "dorm food"! Michael would always reserve some of the ingredients, and in late afternoon when the main work was finished, he would show us how to "do something really special" with them. The only disappointment was that we then had to wolf our "project" down at about 4:50 p.m., just before the crowd arrived, whereas the food and the presentation deserved an elegant setting, good wine, candlelight, a later start, and some leisure.

I've always been grateful for the two great educations-for-life that Eastman gave me: in the studios, concert halls, and library; and in the kitchen.

1   Preheat the oven to 300°F.

2   Melt the butter and stir in the salt, cinnamon, and cayenne. In a bowl, toss together the pecans and butter mixture.

3   Spread the nuts on a baking sheet, and roast for 15 minutes. Cool completely. (The nuts can be made up to a week in advance and stored in an airtight container.)

4   Combine the dressing ingredients in a small jar and shake until emulsified.

5   Toss the salad ingredients, dressing, and spiced pecans together just before serving.

YIELD: 8 servings

— *Jeffrey Stokes*

SPICED PECANS:

3 tablespoons unsalted butter

1 teaspoon salt

1 teaspoon ground cinnamon

¼ teaspoon cayenne

1⅔ cups shelled pecans

DRESSING:

2 tablespoons sherry vinegar

1 tablespoon Dijon mustard

½ cup olive oil

Salt and pepper to taste

SALAD:

1 head Boston lettuce, torn

1 head red leaf lettuce, torn

2 Red Delicious apples, cored and cubed

½ pound feta cheese, crumbled

Quick Beef Stroganoff

1 Cut the beef into julienne strips. Season with salt, pepper, and paprika.

2 In a large skillet, melt the butter over medium-high heat until the foam subsides. Sauté the beef strips, in batches if necessary, until just medium-rare. Remove the meat from the skillet and set aside. Do not drain the fat.

3 Reduce the heat to medium and, in the same skillet, sauté the onion until translucent. Add the mushrooms and sauté until the mushrooms are softened. Add more butter if necessary.

4 Sprinkle the flour over the mushrooms. Reduce the heat to medium-low and cook, stirring, for a minute or two.

5 Gradually stir in about 2 cups of the sour cream. Add up to 1 cup more sour cream or milk, in whatever proportions you like, to achieve the volume and consistency desired. Stir in the ketchup, nutmeg, and Worcestershire sauce.

6 Return the meat to the pan, stirring to coat, and gently heat through.

7 Serve over toast, rice, or (my choice) broad egg noodles.

YIELD: 4 to 6 servings

— *Jeffrey Stokes*

1½ pounds sirloin or other beef for grilling

Salt, pepper, and paprika to taste

2 tablespoons butter

2 tablespoons finely chopped onion

½ pound mushrooms, sliced

1 scant tablespoon all-purpose flour

2 to 3 cups sour cream*

1 tablespoon ketchup

½ teaspoon nutmeg

½ teaspoon Worcestershire sauce

*For a thinner sauce, substitute milk for some of the sour cream, or use low-fat sour cream.

Vegetable Rice to Serve with Any Curry

1   In a large saucepan, bring the water to a boil over high heat. Stir in the rice, cinnamon stick, bay leaves, cloves, cardamom pods, and salt. Return to a boil; this should take less than a minute. Stir, cover tightly, reduce the heat to low, and cook for 5 minutes. Stir in the cauliflower, peas, and green beans. Cook for 5 minutes more. Stir again, and if the rice looks too dry, or is sticking to the bottom of the pot, add a splash or two more water. If it looks too wet, stir and cook on low heat a few minutes longer. Remove the cinnamon stick, bay leaves, cloves, and cardamom pods.

2   Cover again, reduce the heat to the lowest setting or turn off entirely. The rice will stay warm for some time if you resist the urge to lift the lid and check.

3   In a large wok or skillet, heat the vegetable oil over medium heat. Add the onion and cook, stirring frequently, for 5 minutes, until lightly browned. Add the prunes. Cook for a minute or two until they are a bit puffy. Add the rice mixture and the carrots. Cook, stirring, until heated through, adding a little more oil if necessary to prevent sticking.

4   Transfer to a serving dish, sprinkle with slivered almonds and garnish with tomato wedges, cucumber slices, radishes, and slivered green onions. At the table, pass crushed peanuts, grated coconut, dried chili flakes, and banana slices as additional garnishes.

YIELD: 4 to 6 servings

— *Jeffrey Stokes*

1½ cups water

1½ cups long-grain rice

1 cinnamon stick

2 bay leaves

6 whole cloves

2 whole green cardamom pods

1 teaspoon salt

1 cup thawed frozen cauliflower florets*

1 cup thawed frozen peas*

½ cup thawed frozen green beans*

¼ cup vegetable oil

1 large onion, thinly sliced

1 cup pitted prunes or raisins, rinsed and dried

1 cup finely grated carrots

Slivered almonds

Various garnishes (see instructions)

*If you use fresh vegetables instead of frozen, blanch or microwave until crisp-tender before adding to the rice.

TSUYOSHI TSUTSUMI
Cello

Cellist Tsuyoshi Tsutsumi won the International Casals Competition in Budapest in 1963. Born in Tokyo, his early training led him to his debut at the age of 12 with the Tokyo Philharmonic, performing the Saint-Saëns concerto. A Fulbright Foundation grant took him to the United States to study at Indiana University. Currently, Tsuyoshi is on the faculty of Indiana University as professor of music. He was elected the first President of the Japan Cello Society and is the Music Director of Kirishima International Music Festival and President of Suntory Music Foundation.

Orange Chicken Tsutsumi

1 Preheat the oven to 350°F.

2 Sprinkle oregano inside the chicken thighs. Roll up each chicken thigh around a ham slice and a celery stick. Place the four rolls in a small baking dish. Drizzle with the mustard and soy sauce. Pour the orange juice over the chicken rolls.

3 Bake for 35 to 45 minutes, or until the chicken is cooked through. (Or microwave, loosely covered, for 7 to 8 minutes.)

4 Place orange slices on each chicken roll. Sprinkle with Cointreau (if using).

5 Serve on a bed of rice with pan juices spooned over top. Sprinkle with chopped fresh parsley.

YIELD: 4 servings

— *Tsuyoshi Tsutsumi*

4 boneless skinless chicken thighs

Dried oregano

4 thin slices ham, cut to size of each thigh

4 pieces celery, cut to size of chicken

2 teaspoons prepared mustard

2 teaspoons soy sauce

½ cup orange juice

1 orange, sliced

Cointreau (optional)

Chopped fresh parsley, for garnish

Nutty Wild Rice Salad

CHRISTINE VLAJK
Viola

Christine Vlajk is the viola player with the Penderecki String Quartet. The quartet, founded in Poland in 1986 with the support of Krzysztof Penderecki, Poland's foremost composer, has become one of the most celebrated chamber ensembles in the music world. The quartet is a devoted champion of the music of our time and has commissioned new quartets from a number of Canadian composers. The Penderecki String Quartet is Quartet-in-Residence at Wilfrid Laurier University and devotes much of its time to Quartetfest, an intensive spring-term seminar at WLU.

Here is one of my all-time favourite recipes. There is a sense of the exotic because of the wild rice, and lovely variety from the crunchiness of the veggies and nuts. It's always a hit at parties.

1 In a medium saucepan, cover the rice with cold water to a depth of 1 inch above the rice. Bring to a boil. Drain the rice, return it to the pot, and add the stock. Simmer, covered, until the stock is absorbed, about 1 hour.

2 In a medium bowl, whisk together all of the dressing ingredients. Add the warm rice and toss it with the dressing. Cool.

3 Add the peas, peppers, almonds, and green onions to the rice. Toss well. Refrigerate at least 2 hours.

4 Serve in small lettuce cups or in a lettuce-lined bowl.

YIELD: 4 servings

— *Christine Vlajk*

½ cup wild rice

2 cups beef stock

1 cup thawed frozen peas

¾ cup chopped red peppers, celery, or any crunchy vegetable

¼ cup slivered almonds, toasted

4 green onions, sliced

Lettuce cups

DRESSING:

¼ cup vegetable oil

2 tablespoons red wine vinegar

1 tablespoon soy sauce

2 teaspoons sesame oil

1 teaspoon brown sugar or maple syrup

1 clove garlic, minced (optional)

DOROTHEA VOGEL
Viola

Dorothea Vogel is the violist with the Allegri String Quartet, founded fifty years ago when four remarkably talented players came together to create inspired performances of the great classical and Romantic chamber music repertoire. England's most respected quartet today derives both continuity and individuality from its members, who are the proud guardians of those original ideals. Dorothea Vogel has also appeared as a soloist with the Zurich Kammerorchester and at London's Wigmore Hall. She teaches at Pro Corda, a school for young chamber music players in England. Her viola is by J.B. Vuillaume.

Easy Bread

This recipe makes the most delicious bread with no effort. If you use more flour, the bread will be more solid; less, it will be softer. The best way to find out is by trial and error.

1. In a large bowl, mix all the ingredients with a spoon until a dough forms. Cover the dough with plastic wrap and leave overnight in a warm place, such as an oven with the light on.

2. Preheat the oven to 350°F. Grease 2 loaf pans with olive oil.

3. Divide the dough in half, shape into 2 loaves, and put it in the loaf pans.

4. Bake for 1 hour, or until the loaf sounds hollow when tapped on the bottom. Turn loaves out of pans and cool on a rack.

YIELD: 2 loaves

— *Dorothea Vogel*

8 cups all-purpose flour (approximate), or substitute 2 cups whole wheat flour for part

1 tablespoon salt

A pinch of fresh or active dry yeast

1 tablespoon live-culture yogurt

2½ cups warm water

A handful sunflower seeds, or any other you fancy

Peppered Strawberries

JASPER WOOD
Violin

Jasper Wood is one of the finest violinists of his generation and one of North America's fastest-rising stars. He was born in Canada in 1974, gave his first public performance at the age of five, and has since received rave reviews for his performances throughout North America. An avid chamber musician, he has performed with various ensembles throughout the world, ranging from baroque to contemporary. He performs on a 1700 Taft Stradivarius violin on loan from the Canada Council for the Arts and an anonymous donor. Jasper and Grace were married in the summer of 2005.

The following is one of my favourite recipes for many reasons.

When I first met my girlfriend, now my wife, and was trying to win over her heart, I invited her to my place for a romantic dinner. I planned a good meal, but it needed to end with a flare. The first thing that came to mind was Peppered Strawberries. I first tried this amazing dessert at the Windjammer restaurant at the Delta Beausejour in my hometown of Moncton, New Brunswick. This was a perfect recipe for our evening together. This dessert is a flambé, so fire is involved. To be impressive the room should be on the darker side, a good excuse for dimming the lights! Grace was really impressed, and made me promise to never make this dessert for another girl!

For this recipe to work best, I suggest using a gas stove. However, if you don't have one, use a lighter or match, and make sure you have your technique down for lighting the flambé. Nothing can ruin the mood more than a cook who is scared to light the fire. Also, I highly suggest using a stainless steel frying pan rather than nonstick.

1 Scoop ice cream into 2 individual dessert dishes. Place them in the freezer.

2 Melt the butter and sugar in a large (not nonstick) skillet over low heat. Stir in the strawberries. Add the pepper, giving your pepper mill 10 to 12 turns.

3 Cook the strawberries, always stirring and mixing in a stylish way, until they become slightly cooked. You don't want the strawberries to be either mushy or raw.

(continued on next page)

Vanilla ice cream (all-natural makes a difference)

1 tablespoon unsalted butter

1 tablespoon sugar

1 cup fresh local strawberries, larger ones cut into halves or quarters (You don't want the strawberries to be too small or thin.)

Freshly ground medium-coarse pepper to taste

2 tablespoons (or more) Grand Marnier

4   Pour the Grand Marnier over the strawberries, and ignite by tipping the skillet until the flame from your gas stove, match, or lighter touches the juice of the strawberries. Your food will now catch on fire. Be careful here! Once the flame has stopped burning, quickly pour the strawberries over the ice cream.

5   If you prefer your syrup to be thicker, or if you have too much syrup, remove the strawberries with a slotted spoon and continue to cook the syrup until it reduces to your liking.

YIELD: 2 servings

— *Jasper Wood*

Festive Baked Brie

SIMON WYNBERG
Guitar

Simon Wynberg is not only a virtuoso performer of distinction but one of the guitar's foremost scholars, researching many areas of the instrument's neglected repertory, much of which he has recorded. He enjoys a diverse career as soloist, chamber musician, accompanist, producer, and arranger. He is currently Artistic Director of ARC, the Royal Conservatory of Music's faculty ensemble-in-residence. He enjoys single-malt Scotch, *The Sopranos,* and the writing of Mordecai Richler.

Here is something most people love to eat. It is perfect for a party but definitely not low in fat. It is also the perfect dish for the challenged male—someone like me whose culinary skills do not extend much beyond correctly identifying the larger kitchen appliances. Fortunately this dish needs practically no expertise—praise and admiration are inversely proportional to the required effort and ability. It's rather like an extremely impressive piece of music, which sounds almost as good when played by an accomplished grade three student. My wife, Robyn, who is a virtuoso in the kitchen, first led me through this recipe.

1 In a small skillet over medium heat, melt the butter. Add the almonds and cook, stirring occasionally, for a few minutes, until the almonds start to brown. Pour the almonds onto a paper towel and cool to room temperature.

2 Preheat the oven to 350°F. Lightly grease a cookie sheet.

3 With a sharp paring knife, trim the rind off the top of the cheese, leaving the side and bottom intact. Sprinkle the almonds on top of the Brie. Add a dash of pepper.

4 Using a floured rolling pin and working on a floured surface, roll out the puff pastry into a circle large enough to completely wrap the Brie. Carefully lay the pastry over the Brie and almonds. Using a pancake flipper if required, fold the pastry under the cheese and seal off all exposed rind on the side and bottom. Place the wrapped cheese, almond side up, on the cookie sheet.

(continued on next page)

3 tablespoons unsalted butter

1 (2-ounce/50 gram) packet chopped blanched almonds

1 (16-ounce/450 gram) round of Brie

Freshly ground pepper to taste

1 package frozen puff pastry, thawed

1 egg, beaten

Fresh bread, crackers, grapes, and apple wedges

5   Using a sharp knife, cut an attractive slit design in the pastry top to allow the heat to escape. With a pastry brush, paint the sides and top of the cheese with the beaten egg. (At this point the cheese can be wrapped in plastic wrap and kept in the fridge for a week before cooking.)

6   Bake in the middle of the oven for 25 minutes, or until golden brown. Carefully slide the Brie onto a large platter.

7   Serve piping hot with fresh bread, crackers, grapes and apple wedges.

— *Simon Wynberg*

Pasta with Pesto

These days we seldom eat carbs, so pasta is a treat. We have pesto on special occasions. A first dinner at home, after being away performing, is a celebration, and pesto is often on the menu. My wife Amanda's mother, Lesley, makes the best pesto in the world. It's very garlicky, which keeps us all healthy, and it's not too oily either.

If your garlic is beginning to sprout, make sure you cut out the shoot. It can taste bitter.

1 For the pesto, very gently warm the cashews in a nonstick pan over medium heat for a minute or so. Place the cashews, garlic, salt, and freshly ground pepper in a food processor, and give it a quick buzz. Add all the basil and turn on the processor. Slowly pour in the oil, using just enough to bring the mixture to a thickish paste. You should not see the oil.

2 Remove the pesto from the processor and stir in the ½ cup of cheese. Cover the pesto with a very thin layer of oil. This will keep the colour bright green.

3 Cook the pasta in lots and lots of boiling salted water. When al dente, drain the pasta, reserving 1 cup of the cooking water.

4 Put the pasta in a big, warmed bowl. Add ½ cup cooking water and then the pesto. Add more water if necessary. Stir until the pasta is well coated with sauce. Add more oil if you think it really needs it. Sprinkle with freshly ground pepper and a good handful of cheese and serve immediately. Pass extra cheese in a separate bowl.

YIELD: 6 servings

— *Pinchas Zuckerman*

PINCHAS ZUKERMAN
Violin

Pinchas Zukerman has been recognized as a phenomenon for nearly four decades, his musical genius and prodigious technique long a marvel to critics and audiences. His devotion to younger generations of musicians who are inspired by his magnetism has been applauded worldwide. Equally respected as a violinist, violist, conductor, pedagogue, and chamber musician, he is indeed a master of our time. Pinchas Zukerman is the Music Director of the National Arts Centre Orchestra of Canada.

PESTO:

12 large salted cashews, or more to taste

6 to 10 large cloves garlic (purple-skinned variety), peeled and split

Salt and freshly ground pepper to taste

Leaves from 2 or 3 large bunches of basil

Best-quality virgin olive oil (I don't know the measurement, but be conservative.)

½ cup freshly grated Parmigiano-Reggiano cheese

PASTA:

1½ pounds Italian fusilli or other curly pasta that will trap the sauce

Freshly ground pepper to taste

1 cup freshly grated Parmigiano-Reggiano cheese

Keyboard & Percussion

Ann Airton and Brian Newbould, *piano*
James Anagnoson and Leslie Kinton, *piano duo*
John Arpin, *piano*
Rian de Waal, *piano,* and Marion van den Akker, *mezzo-soprano*
Gene DiNovi, *piano*
Craig Harley, *piano*
Michael Jarvis, *harpsichord*
Beverly Johnston, *percussion*
Michel Lambert, *percussion*
Stéphane Lemelin, *piano*
Glen Montgomery, *piano*
Stéphan Sylvestre, *piano*
Alexander Tselyakov, *piano*

Lentil and Cashew Bake

ANN AIRTON, *Piano*
BRIAN NEWBOULD, *Piano*

Ann Airton studied with
Vivian Langrish at the Royal
Academy of Music in London,
where she won the Andrew Sykes
Open Scholarship and gained
the LRAM performer's diploma
at the age of 17. In concert
work throughout Britain, she has
appeared as soloist, accompanist,
and duo-partner with Brian
Newbould. Brian is the author
of major studies of Schubert.
His performing versions of
sketched symphonies and other
works left unfinished by Schubert
have been widely performed.
Brian is a professor of music at
the University of Hull.

Vegetarians visiting the Festival will soon discover that they are provided for at the Bay Street Café. Those who stop over in Toronto must seek out Le Commensal, well placed in the central area, where they will find a vast buffet of vegetarian dishes.

1 Preheat the oven to 375°F. Grease a small casserole dish.

2 Rinse the lentils, place them in a saucepan, cover with water, and cook for 15 to 20 minutes, until soft. Drain.

3 In the same saucepan, heat the oil over medium heat. Add the onion and celery, and cook, stirring occasionally, until the onion is transparent. Add the tomatoes and cook for a further 5 minutes.

4 Remove from the heat and add the drained lentils, the cashews, bread crumbs, yeast extract, herb seasoning, garlic, and egg. Stir to combine.

5 Turn the mixture into the casserole dish. Bake for 30 minutes, or until soft and browned on top. Serve with your favourite sauce.

6 May be frozen for up to 3 months, thawed for 3 hours, and cooked for 20 minutes (or 10 minutes in the microwave).

YIELD: 4 servings

— *Ann Airton and Brian Newbould*

¾ cup lentils

1 tablespoon corn oil

1 small onion, chopped

1 stalk celery, chopped

1 cup peeled and chopped tomatoes (about 6 tomatoes)

½ cup ground cashew nuts

⅓ cup fresh whole-wheat bread crumbs

2 teaspoons yeast extract (Marmite or Vegemite)

1 teaspoon mixed herb seasoning

1 clove garlic, crushed

1 egg

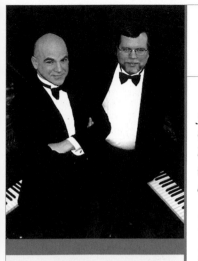

JAMES ANAGNOSON AND LESLIE KINTON
Piano Duo

Since their Wigmore Hall debut in 1976, James Anagnoson and Leslie Kinton have set the standard for duo-piano artistry in Canada, establishing at the same time an enviable international reputation. Jim is a graduate of the Eastman School of Music and holds a master's degree from the Juilliard School. Leslie was a scholarship student at the Royal Conservatory of Music and holds a master's degree in theory and musicology from the University of Toronto. Both are currently on the faculty of the Royal Conservatory of Music's Glenn Gould School.

Baily's Sticky Buns

Jim is originally from Boston, and so we spend many summers in Cape Cod. We became great friends with Baily Ruckert, who had a bed and breakfast in Cahoon Hollow. Baily made the best breakfasts in the world without a doubt. This is one of her recipes, very simple and a big hit!

1 Preheat the oven to 350°F. Grease a Bundt pan.

2 Sprinkle half of the pecans in the bottom of the Bundt pan.

3 In a small saucepan, combine the brown sugar, butter, water, and remaining pecans. Bring the mixture to a boil, stirring, and boil for 1 minute.

4 Pour half of this mixture over the pecans in the pan.

5 Slice each roll of crescent dough into 8 slices. (Do not unroll the dough.) Arrange 8 slices over the brown sugar mixture in the pan. Sprinkle with half the raisins and half the cinnamon.

6 Place the remaining dough slices on top of the others. Pour the remaining brown sugar mixture over top. Sprinkle with the remaining raisins and cinnamon.

7 Bake for 25 minutes, or until golden brown. Cool on a rack for 10 minutes. Invert the pan onto a plate to unmould the buns.

YIELD: 4 to 6 servings

— Jim Anagnoson

½ cup chopped pecans

1 cup packed light brown sugar

½ cup butter or margarine

2 tablespoons water

2 (8-ounce/235 gram) tubes refrigerated crescent rolls

½ cup raisins

1 teaspoon cinnamon

Blueberry Tart

This is a perfect summer recipe. The crust can be made a day ahead.

1 For the crust, put the flour, sugar and butter into a food processor. Pulse to mix. Add the vinegar, then pulse just until the pastry forms a ball. Do not overmix.

2 Pat the pastry into the bottom and up the sides of a 10-inch tart pan with a removable bottom. Cover and chill for at least 2 hours.

3 Preheat the oven to 350°F.

4 For the filling, combine the sugar, flour, cinnamon, and 2½ cups of the blueberries. Pour the mixture into the chilled crust. Bake for 45 minutes, or until the filling bubbles. Cool.

5 Remove the rim from the tart pan. Spread the remaining 1 cup of blueberries over the tart and sprinkle with a little confectioners' sugar.

YIELD: 6 to 8 servings

— *Jim Anagnoson*

CRUST:

1 cup all-purpose flour

2 tablespoons granulated sugar

½ cup butter

1 tablespoon white vinegar

FILLING:

⅔ cup granulated sugar

2 tablespoons flour

¼ teaspoon cinnamon

3½ cups wild blueberries, rinsed and dried

Confectioners' sugar, for decoration

Spicy Shrimp

This recipe is from our yoga teacher, Lisa Schwartz, who is an amazing teacher and cook. It is called "spicy" shrimp, but if you just add a small amount of the chili flakes, it is not spicy, just very flavourful.

1. In a large bowl, combine the shrimp, coriander, salt, chili flakes, turmeric, cumin, and garlic. Let stand 1 hour.

2. Heat the oil in a large skillet over medium-high heat. Add the spiced shrimp, and sauté just until they turn pink, 2 or 3 minutes. Remove from the heat and toss with the lemon juice and chives. Serve immediately.

YIELD: 4 to 6 servings

— *Jim Anagnoson*

2 pounds shrimp, peeled and deveined

2 teaspoons ground coriander

1 teaspoon salt

1 teaspoon dried chili flakes, or to taste

1 teaspoon turmeric

1 teaspoon ground cumin

2 cloves garlic, minced

¼ cup vegetable oil

Juice of 2 lemons

2 tablespoons finely chopped chives

Carrot Cake

JOHN ARPIN
Piano

Pianist John Arpin has long been regarded as one of the most versatile performers on the Canadian music scene. This talented artist composes, arranges, conducts, records, and maintains a full concert schedule. Though he plays everything from turn-of-the-century classics to jazz to Broadway show tunes, John Arpin's name has become synonymous with piano rags, and he is respected as one of the top ragtime musicians in the world today. In 1998 he received the Scott Joplin Award in recognition of his extraordinary contributions to the field of ragtime.

Since I am not really a huge cook, I am offering my favourite recipe that my wife, Mary Jane, makes for me. It turns out perfectly every time.

1 Preheat the oven to 350°F. Grease and flour two 8-inch-round cake pans.

2 Sift together the flour, granulated sugar, cinnamon, baking soda, and salt.

3 In a large bowl, beat the eggs until frothy. Slowly beat in the oil. Gradually add the flour mixture, beating until smooth. Stir in the carrots and nuts.

4 Pour the batter into the cake pans. Bake for 35 to 45 minutes, or until a toothpick inserted into the centre of the cake comes out clean. Remove from the pans and cool on a rack.

5 For the frosting, beat the cream cheese until fluffy. Add the butter, milk, and confectioners' sugar, beating after each addition. Continue to beat until the desired consistency for spreading is reached. After icing the cake, place it in the refrigerator to set for 15 minutes or so.

6 Decorate as desired.

YIELD: a large two-layer cake, about 12 servings

— *John Arpin*

CAKE

2 cups all-purpose flour

2 cups granulated sugar

2 teaspoons cinnamon

2 teaspoons baking soda

1 teaspoon salt

4 eggs

1 cup vegetable oil

4 cups grated carrots

½ cup chopped pecans or walnuts

FROSTING

1 (8-ounce/250 gram) package cream cheese, softened

¼ pound butter, softened or melted (½ cup)

¼ to ½ cup milk

2 to 3 cups confectioners' sugar

Gold Medal Pasta Salad

RIAN DE WAAL, *Piano*
MARION VAN DEN AKKER,
Mezzo-soprano

Rian de Waal is internationally acclaimed as the Netherlands' most important pianist. He has performed on all the most important stages in Europe, North America, and the Far East in recital and as soloist with major orchestras. He is founder and Artistic Director of the Rhijnauwen Chamber Music Festival in Bunnik and of chamber music festivals in Zwolle and Sittard. Mezzo-soprano Marion van den Akker is an opera singer, soloist, and chamber music performer. She has performed widely throughout North America and Europe, has given lieder recitals in more than nine languages, and is professor of classical singing at the North Netherlands Conservatoire.

This recipe originated when Marion suddenly remembered, at the last minute, that she was supposed to enter a cooking contest at her daughter's school. She frantically threw some ingredients together and rushed the salad over to the school. To her dismay, she saw that the other mothers had garnished their entries to look like works of art, while hers looked rather mundane in its bowl. You can imagine her surprise and delight when her salad won the Gold Medal!

1 In a large pot of boiling water with the fish bouillon cubes, cook the pasta until al dente. Drain and let cool. Transfer to a large serving bowl.

2 Drain the tuna and break it into small pieces. Add the tuna, peas and carrots, and sour cream to the pasta. Toss well. Season with salt, pepper, and lemon juice.

3 Finely chop the dill and sprinkle over top.

YIELD: 4 to 6 servings

— *Rian de Waal and Marion van den Akker*

1 pound pasta shells

3 fish bouillon cubes*

6⅓ cups water

2 (6-ounce/170 gram) cans tuna

1 cup thawed frozen or drained canned peas and carrots

½ cup sour cream

Salt and freshly ground pepper to taste

Lemon juice to taste

1 bunch fresh dill

*If you are unable to find fish bouillon cubes, you might try vegetable bouillon cubes together with the liquid from the canned tuna.

Penne con Vongole for Two

GENE DiNOVI
Piano

Pianist Gene DiNovi was born in Brooklyn and grew up in New York City. At the age of 16, he was asked by Dizzy Gillespie to sit in with his band. Over the years, he has been pianist and arranger for Benny Goodman and Buddy Rich and recorded with Artie Shaw. In the early 1970s, Gene DiNovi decided to settle in Toronto and has developed quite a large following. Gene DiNovi's work *Alice in the Orchestra* premiered at the 2002 Festival of the Sound.

1 Scrub the clams carefully several times. Rinse them well. Put the cleaned clams and 1 cup of the wine into a saucepan with a tight-fitting lid. Bring to a boil, reduce the heat, and simmer until the clams have opened. Using a slotted spoon, immediately transfer the clams to a bowl. Discard any clams that did not open. Strain the cooking liquid through a fine strainer lined with cheesecloth, reserving the liquid.

2 Set aside 8 clams in their shells. Separate the remaining clams from their shells.

3 In a large, heavy-bottomed saucepan over medium heat, cook the onion in the olive oil until it's soft and golden, about 10 minutes. Stir in the garlic.

4 Meanwhile, cook the penne in a large pot of boiling salted water until al dente. *Do not overcook the pasta, because it will get a second cooking in the clam sauce.* As soon as the pasta is ready, drain, and toss with the butter.

5 Bring the onions to a sizzle over high heat and add the tomato. As the tomatoes break down, add the remaining ½ cup of wine and the reserved clam liquid. Reduce the heat to low and add the pasta and all the clams to the sauce. Toss with the parsley. Cover and simmer for 15 to 20 minutes, while eating antipasta. *Buon appetito!*

YIELD: 2 to 4 servings

ANTIPASTA SUGGESTION: a jar of marinated artichokes, salami, prosciutto, and mozzarella slices. Drizzle with olive oil, and scatter with fresh parsley and olives.

— *Gene DiNovi*

2 pounds fresh clams in the shell

1½ cups dry white wine (preferably the wine you will be drinking)

1 large red onion, finely chopped

2 tablespoons olive oil

2 cloves garlic, minced (We often add more, since we are a family where there is no such rule as too much garlic!)

2 cups penne

1 tablespoon unsalted butter

1 large beefsteak tomato, seeded and chopped

¼ cup chopped fresh parsley

Raspberry Swirl Cheesecake

CRAIG HARLEY
Piano

Craig Harley, a native of Parry Sound, began playing the piano at a young age. In 1993, he moved to Toronto to attend the University of Toronto's jazz program, from which he graduated in 1997. Since then he has performed in many music festivals and at several Toronto clubs. Craig Harley has arranged music on several CDs and is a member of a cooperative Canadian independent record label, The Breath Records.

Cheesecake has always been a favourite of mine. This outstanding recipe is my mother-in-law's. Hope you like it as much as I do!

1 Preheat the oven to 300°F. Grease a 9-inch springform pan.

2 In a small bowl, blend the crumbs, butter, and sugar. Press the mixture firmly into the bottom of the pan.

3 In a large mixing bowl, beat the cream cheese until fluffy. Gradually stir in the condensed milk, beating until smooth. Beat in the eggs and the lemon juice.

4 Pour half of the batter into the prepared pan and spread it evenly. Drop ¼ can of the pie filling in small spoonfuls over the batter. Repeat the procedure with the remaining batter and another ¼ can of the pie filling. To create a ripple effect, swirl a knife through the batter from one side of the pan to the other.

5 Bake for 45 to 50 minutes, or until tester comes out clean.

6 Add the liqueur to the remaining ½ can of the pie filling. Chill if desired. Serve the sauce with the cheesecake.

YIELD: 10 to 12 servings

— Craig Harley

1¼ cups graham wafer crumbs

⅓ cup butter, melted

¼ cup sugar

2 (8-ounce/250 gram) packages cream cheese, softened

1 (10-ounce/300 mL) can sweetened condensed milk

3 large eggs

¼ cup lemon juice

1 (16-ounce/454 mL) can raspberry pie filling

2 tablespoons orange or raspberry liqueur, or water

Cold Curried Chicken

MICHAEL JARVIS
Harpsichord

Acclaimed as one of Canada's finest harpsichordists, fortepianists, and continuo players, Michael Jarvis has performed with some of Canada's leading orchestras and chamber ensembles and is Artistic Director of the Baroque Players of Hamilton. He is Director of Music at St. Joseph's Church in Hamilton and Conductor of the Mohawk College Singers, and teaches harpsichord at Wilfrid Laurier University and Havergal College.

1 Heat the oil in a saucepan over medium heat. Fry the onion gently for 5 minutes or until it is soft. Stir in the curry powder and cook a few minutes more to bring out the flavour.

2 Add the stock, chutney, tomato paste, and lemon juice. Stir until the mixture begins to boil. Reduce the heat and simmer for 5 minutes.

3 Remove from the heat and transfer the sauce to a bowl. Allow the sauce to cool. Stir in the mayonnaise and cream.

4 Remove the meat from the chicken in chunky or bite-sized pieces, and arrange in a single layer on a serving dish. Spoon the curry mayonnaise sauce over the chicken. Refrigerate until serving time.

YIELD: 4 to 6 servings

— *Michael Jarvis*

1 tablespoon olive oil

1 small onion, finely chopped

1 tablespoon curry powder (at least)

½ cup chicken stock

2 tablespoons sweet chutney

1 rounded teaspoon tomato paste

Juice of ½ lemon

1 cup mayonnaise (not Miracle Whip!)

3 tablespoons heavy cream

1 chicken, cooked and cooled

Moroccan Braised Lamb

BEVERLEY JOHNSTON
Percussion

A charismatic performer and an outstanding musician, Canada's premier percussionist, Beverley Johnston, is internationally recognized for her virtuosic and dynamic performances on a wide range of percussion instruments. Her exciting performances have been distinguished as unconventional, effectively combining classical transcriptions, contemporary music, and a touch of theatre. Over the years, she has commissioned and performed several works by leading Canadian composers, and some of these works have become a staple of the percussion repertory around the world.

This meal takes a long time to make but it's worth it!

1   In a saucepan, simmer the chickpeas in the water, partially covered, for 1¼ hours, or until tender. Remove from the heat and let stand for 2 hours.

2   Meanwhile, in a small bowl macerate the raisins in sherry for 2 hours.

3   Meanwhile, in a large bowl marinate the lamb in the orange juice and garlic, covered and refrigerated, stirring occasionally, for 1½ hours. Remove from the fridge and continue to marinate the lamb, covered, at room temperature, for 30 minutes more. Drain the lamb, discarding the marinade, and pat dry.

4   Preheat the oven to 400°F.

5   In an 8-quart heavy kettle, heat the oil over medium-high heat until hot but not smoking. Brown the lamb in batches, transferring it with tongs to a plate as browned.

6   Add the carrots and onion, and cook, stirring, until softened, about 2 minutes. Add the lamb, almonds, cumin, cinnamon, coriander, thyme, saffron, wine, and the raisin mixture.

7   Drain the chickpeas and stir them into the lamb mixture with the tomatoes, olives, lemon zest, lemon juice, and salt and pepper.

(continued on next page)

½ cup dried chickpeas, picked over

3½ cups water

½ cup raisins

½ cup dry sherry

3 pounds boneless leg of lamb, cut into 1-inch cubes

1 cup freshly squeezed orange juice

4 cloves garlic, minced

½ cup olive oil

2 carrots, chopped

1 onion, chopped

½ cup sliced blanched almonds

1½ teaspoons ground cumin

1½ teaspoons cinnamon

1 teaspoon ground coriander

½ teaspoon dried thyme, crumbled

¼ teaspoon saffron threads, crumbled

½ cup dry red wine

CHRISTOS HATZIS

8 Braise the lamb, covered, in the middle of the oven for 2 hours, or until the lamb is very tender.

9 Serve lamb with the couscous.

YIELD: 6 servings

— *Bev Johnston*

2¼ cups canned whole tomatoes, including juice, coarsely chopped

½ cup pitted Kalamata olives

Zest of 1 lemon

2 tablespoons fresh lemon juice

Salt and pepper to taste

Accompaniment: cooked couscous

Zucchini Crescent Pie

I found this recipe many years ago and have continued to make it. Serve it with your favourite salad and crusty bread. It also goes well with sausages on the side.

1 Preheat the oven to 375°F.

2 In a 10-inch skillet, melt the butter over medium heat. Cook the zucchini and the onion until tender. Remove from the heat and stir in the parsley, salt, pepper, basil, oregano, and garlic powder.

3 In a large bowl, beat the eggs. Stir in the cheese. Stir the egg mixture into the vegetable mixture.

4 Separate the dough into 8 triangles. Line an ungreased 11-inch quiche pan, a 10-inch pie pan, or a 12 by 8-inch baking dish with the dough, pressing it over the bottom and up the sides of the pan to form a pie shell. Spread the mustard over the dough. Pour the vegetable mixture evenly into pie shell.

5 Bake the pie for 18 to 20 minutes, or until a knife inserted near the centre comes out clean. (If the crust becomes too brown, cover it with foil during last 10 minutes of baking.)

6 Let the pie stand 10 minutes before serving. Serve hot.

YIELD: 6 servings

— *Bev Johnston*

½ cup butter or margarine

3 medium zucchini, thinly sliced (about 4 cups)

1 large onion, coarsely chopped (about 1 cup)

½ cup chopped fresh parsley (or 2 tablespoons parsley flakes)

½ teaspoon salt

½ teaspoon black pepper

½ teaspoon dried basil

¼ teaspoon dried oregano

¼ teaspoon garlic powder

2 eggs

8 ounces shredded Muenster or mozzarella cheese (2 cups)

1 (8-ounce/235 gram) tube refrigerated crescent rolls

2 teaspoons Dijon or prepared mustard

Spinach Gratin

MICHEL LAMBERT
Percussion

Percussionist Michel Lambert is the descendant of a virtual dynasty of classical musicians in Quebec. His fascination with drums and composition inspired him to pursue his musical education at Berklee College in Boston. He has composed several orchestral works and has produced a number of paintings, including a commission from the Canada Council to illustrate the four-CD boxed set of a compilation of Canadian music to celebrate the fiftieth anniversary of the United Nations.

Michel has performed jazz drums at the Festival of the Sound many times over the past few years, and always enjoys the delicious fish in the area. Here's a recipe to accompany your fish or meat dinners, made in Michel's inimitable improvised jazz style—quick and delicious.

When Michel's wife, Jeannette, joins him at the Festival, she always stops to pick up Dutch and German groceries at The Country Gourmet. Originally from the Netherlands and raised in Sudbury, Jeannette finds that visiting Parry Sound and eating dropjes is like returning to two homes! Jeannette has performed with Michel and Dave Young on the outdoor stage on the Parry Sound waterfront, and offers her Dutch variation on the recipe below.

1 Preheat the broiler.

2 Heat the olive oil over high heat in a large skillet or saucepan. Add the garlic and a handful of spinach. Stir in a little of the flour and a pinch of salt.

3 When the spinach has wilted, continue adding portions of spinach, flour, and salt, waiting until the spinach has wilted before adding more, until you have added all the spinach.

4 Add all the milk at once, stirring constantly. Reduce the heat to medium and simmer, stirring, for a few minutes while the sauce thickens.

5 Turn the contents of the pan into a baking dish. Cover with the cheese and sprinkle with nutmeg. Broil until golden. Serve immediately.

YIELD: 2 to 4 servings

— Michel Lambert

2 tablespoons olive oil

1 clove garlic, chopped coarsely

1 bunch or bag fresh spinach, washed and dried

2 tablespoons all-purpose flour

4 or 5 pinches of salt

½ cup milk

¼ pound Gruyère (preferably Swiss or French), shredded

A pinch of nutmeg

VARIATION: Replace the Gruyère with a good aged Gouda or cheddar.

STÉPHANE LEMELIN
Piano

Stéphane Lemelin is a pianist with a broad and eclectic repertoire that ranges from the classical period to the twentieth century and from art-song literature to the Romantic concerto. Since the fall of 2003, he has been a member of Trio Hochelaga, one of Canada's most exciting chamber music ensembles, with violinist Anne Robert and cellist Benoît Loiselle. He is also the Artistic Director of the Prince Edward County Music Festival, a yearly chamber music festival. In 2001, he became professor of music at the University of Ottawa, where he is currently chair of the Department of Music.

Marshmallow Squares

This has been my definition of comfort food since childhood.

1 Preheat the oven to 400°F. Grease a 9-inch square cake pan.

2 In a large bowl, cream together ¼ cup of the butter and 1 cup of the brown sugar. Stir in the egg and mix well.

3 Sift together the flour, baking powder, and salt.

4 Beat half of the flour mixture into the creamed mixture. Beat in ¼ cup of the milk. Beat in the remaining flour mixture. Pour the batter into the cake pan.

5 Bake for 18 to 20 minutes, until firm. As soon as you take the cake out of the oven, cover it with miniature marshmallows. The marshmallows will begin to melt.

6 In a medium saucepan, melt the remaining ¼ cup butter. Stir in the remaining 1 cup brown sugar. Bring to a boil, and cook, stirring occasionally, for 3 minutes. Take the syrup off the heat and add the remaining ¼ cup milk and the confectioners' sugar. Beat the mixture vigorously with a wooden spoon until it starts to lose its shine, 4 or 5 minutes.

7 Pour the caramel mixture over the marshmallow topping. It should set quickly. You may refrigerate the cake to hasten the setting, if desired. Cut into squares and serve warm or at room temperature. The squares keep, covered, for 1 week.

YIELD: 36 squares

— *Stéphane Lemelin*

¼ pound butter (½ cup)

2 cups brown sugar

1 egg, lightly beaten

1 cup all-purpose flour

1 teaspoon baking powder

⅛ teaspoon salt

½ cup milk

3 cups miniature marshmallows

1¼ cups confectioners' sugar

Pecan Squares

GLEN MONTGOMERY
Piano

Pianist Glen Montgomery is a highly respected musician who maintains an active career performing and teaching. In addition to his faculty work, Glen travels extensively, performing as a soloist and in collaboration with chamber musicians. Glen's early music development began with studies on the clarinet with his father and Paul Brodie. At age 11, he was the youngest member of the Toronto Youth Orchestra. Studying with his principal piano teacher, John R. DuVal in Calgary, Glen's first success as a pianist was winning the Alberta Prize Winner's competition at age 16.

These squares are like mini pecan pies.

1. Preheat the oven to 350°F. Grease a 9-inch square cake pan.

2. Sift the flour and confectioners' sugar into a medium bowl. Cut in the softened butter until the mixture resembles fine crumbs. Press the mixture evenly into the prepared pan. Bake for 20 minutes.

3. In a bowl stir together the pecans, melted butter, brown sugar, honey, and cream. Spread the mixture over the baked crust. Bake for 25 minutes more, or until set.

4. Cool completely before cutting into 1½-inch squares. The squares keep, covered, for 1 week.

YIELD: 36 squares

— *Glen Montgomery*

2 cups all-purpose flour

⅔ cup confectioners' sugar

½ pound butter (1 cup), softened

3½ cups chopped pecans

⅓ pound butter (⅔ cup), melted

½ cup brown sugar

½ cup liquid honey

3 tablespoons heavy cream

Ris de Veau Sauce au Porto

STÉPHAN SYLVESTRE
Piano

Pianist Stéphan Sylvestre ranks among the most gifted young Canadian pianists and is in demand as soloist, recitalist, and chamber music player. Critics on both sides of the Atlantic have bestowed lavish praise on his performances. Stéphan holds a master's degree from the Université de Montréal and an artist diploma from the Royal Conservatory of Music in Toronto. He has taught for the Piano Faculty at McGill University as well as Sherbrooke University Music Faculty and has joined the University of Western Ontario Don Wright Faculty of Music.

I was always fond of French cuisine and of giblets. The famous French ris de veau au Porto is one of the few recipes I can make with complete confidence. It is a delicious and refined meal, leaving a good impression with guests invited over for dinner at my home. I can boil an egg and cook ris de veau. What goes between, I do not know!

I recommend a gratin dauphinois and a fresh grilled vegetable of your choice as an accompaniment. Bon appétit à tous!

1   Put the ris de veau in a pot of boiling water mixed with the vinegar, and simmer for 20 minutes.

2   Meanwhile, prepare the demi-glace according to the package instructions. Set aside.

3   Drain the ris de veau and put them in a pie plate. Loosely cover with plastic wrap and set something heavy on top of them. (Scores of the complete Beethoven piano sonatas and Brahms piano trios might be enough, although you might have to add a metronome!) Refrigerate for about 1 hour. This will make them firmer.

4   In a large skillet, melt the butter over medium-high heat. Brown the ris de veau on all sides for a few minutes. Transfer the ris de veau to a warm plate and cover loosely with foil to keep warm.

5   Add the port to the skillet and cook, stirring to scrape up any brown bits. Stir in the demi-glace and let reduce until the sauce is thick enough to coat a spoon. Add a teaspoon of the cream, or more if desired. Season sauce with salt and pepper.

(continued on next page)

1 pound ris de veau (veal sweetbreads)

1 tablespoon vinegar

1 (34 gram) package demi-glace mix*

1 tablespoon unsalted butter

1 cup port

1 teaspoon heavy cream (approximate)

Salt and pepper to taste

*If demi-glace is unavailable, reduce 1 cup veal or chicken stock to about ¼ cup.

6 Pour sauce over sweetbreads and serve immediately.

YIELD: 2 servings

NOTE: This recipe has not been tested because we could not find sweetbreads in Parry Sound. Perhaps these ingredients would be more readily available in a larger centre.

— *Stéphan Sylvestre*

ALEXANDER TSELYAKOV

Piano

Alexander Tselyakov was born into a musical family in Azerbaijan and studied at the Tchaikovsky Conservatory in Moscow with Lev Naumov, custodian of the Heinrich Neuhaus method and credited with producing many extraordinary twentieth-century Russian keyboard masters. Alexander gave his first public performance at the age of nine with the Azerbaijan State Philharmonic Orchestra before going on to win one of the prestigious prizes at the 1986 International Tchaikovsky Competition. He has joined the ranks of Canada's most talented pianists since his Canadian debut at the Ford Centre in 1994.

Blini

Blini is a traditional Russian dish. They are baked in great quantity at Shrove (carnival), the last week before Lent. Blini making was a real sacred mystery. People told fortunes on the dough and kept their blini recipes secret. The first blini were put on windowsills for the poor people and pilgrims. Foreigners were always surprised at how many blini Russians could eat. At Shrove, a mother-in-law must bake a lot of blini for her son-in-law. The most popular blini were made from buckwheat flour. Good blini must be very, very thin. It is said that the thinner your blini are, the more perfect your skill is.

1   Pour the vegetable oil into a saucer. Peel the onion and cut it in half. Stick a fork into one of the onion halves and dip it into the oil. Use this for greasing the griddle.

2   Whisk together the eggs and milk. Add the flour, salt, baking soda, and sugar, and whisk in thoroughly. The dough can be strained so that there are no flour lumps in it.

3   Heat a griddle or skillet over medium-high heat until very hot. Grease the griddle with the onion. Pour a thin layer of batter (about ¼ cup) evenly onto the griddle. Cook until light brown, about 2 minutes on each side. Transfer the blini as they are cooked to a platter and keep them warm, covered with a kitchen towel. Whisk more flour into the batter if you are not successful with thin blini.

4   Blini can be served with butter, sour cream, black or red caviar, fillet of sturgeon, lox, and smoked salmon.

YIELD: 2 to 3 servings

— *Alexander Tselyakov*

2 tablespoons vegetable oil

1 onion

2 large eggs

3 cups milk

1 cup buckwheat flour

A pinch of salt

½ teaspoon baking soda

Sugar to taste

Russian Salad

I have never seen a Russian party without this salad. For Russians it's as traditional as turkey at the Thanksgiving table for Canadian families! And it's so delicious!

1   Cut the potatoes, carrots, onion, dill pickles, and eggs into small cubes. Place in a serving bowl and add the green peas. Cut your choice of meat, fish, or mushrooms into small cubes and add to the vegetable mixture.

2   To make Russian mayonnaise dressing, mix together the mayonnaise, vinegar, and mustard until it becomes smooth and more liquid than real mayo.

3   Combine the Russian dressing with the meat and vegetable mixture.

4   If you wish to decorate the salad, you can boil 3 or 4 eggs, and separate the yolks and the whites. Shape the salad into a rounded cone, like a hill, on a serving dish. Using a very fine shredder, shred the egg yolks onto the top of the "hill." You can also try to make some flowers from the top part of the egg whites and put them on top, so the salad looks like a yellow hill with white flowers on the top! Use your imagination to create even more beautiful designs!

YIELD: 4 to 6 servings

— *Alexander Tselyakov*

4 large potatoes, boiled

2 medium carrots, boiled

1 small red onion

5 medium to large dill pickles

3 hard-boiled eggs

1 cup thawed frozen peas

Ham, smoked turkey breast, smoked pork chops, smoked white fish, or mushrooms

1 cup mayonnaise

2 tablespoons vinegar, or to taste

2 to 5 teaspoons Dijon mustard, to taste

Salad Olivier

This salad is the creation of a French chef, M. Olivier, who, in the 1860s, opened a fashionable restaurant in Moscow called the Hermitage. The present-day version has veered quite far from the original, but Salad Olivier continues to be a favourite hors d'oeuvre and side dish for entrées.

1   Cut the cooked chicken and potatoes into ½-inch cubes. Peel the cucumbers and cut them into ½-inch cubes. In a large bowl, combine the chicken, potatoes, cucumbers, peas, and onion. Add the mayonnaise and mix gently, being careful not to mash any of the ingredients.

2   Refrigerate the salad until serving time (but for no longer than 4 hours). Serve garnished with the eggs, olives, and parsley.

YIELD: serves 8 to 10 as an appetizer, or 6 as an entrée

VARIATION: Vegetable Salad Olivier: omit the chicken or veal to make a delicious meatless side dish.

— Alexander Tselyakov

1 whole chicken breast,* poached, boned, and skinned (or ½ pound cooked lean veal)

1 pound potatoes, boiled in their skins and peeled

2 medium cucumbers in brine (not the same as dill pickles)

1 cup cooked fresh or frozen peas

1 medium onion, finely chopped

1 cup mayonnaise

2 hard-boiled eggs, quartered

8 large Kalamata olives

8 sprigs fresh parsley

* The "whole" chicken breast in this recipe is the two sides of the chicken, and would be the same as 2 chicken breasts bought at a Canadian grocery store.

Benefactors, Composers, Conductors & Directors

Lydia Adams, *conductor*
Margaret Boyd, *executive director*
Carol Campbell, *artistic director's advisor*
James Campbell, *artistic director*
Rona Hokanson, *lecturer*
Anton Kuerti and Kristine Bogyo, *founding artistic directors*
Gary Kulesha, *composer*
Larysa Kuzmenko, *composer*
Charles W. Stockey, *benefactor*

Florence Adams's Fantastic Cape Breton Clam Chowder

LYDIA ADAMS
Conductor

Lydia Adams, one of Canada's most distinguished conductors, is the Artistic Director and Conductor of the Elmer Iseler Singers. Under her direction, the choir has received rave reviews for their Toronto Concert Series and for their extensive touring performances through the U.S. and Canada. Lydia has been invited to conduct the prestigious National Youth Choir of Canada and the Ontario Youth Choir. In addition to conducting the Elmer Iseler Singers, Lydia also conducts the Amadeus Choir of Greater Toronto and is a widely sought guest conductor and clinician.

This is my mom's recipe. It's delicious and easy to make. Back home, after a hard day of Hindemith sonatas, we would all crowd around the table for chowder and crackers. It's also wonderful to have during a snowstorm or on a rainy day.

1 Get your chowder pot out. Melt a blob of butter in it over medium-high heat, and fry up the onions until they're translucent. Add the potatoes to the pot. Add water just to cover the potatoes. Boil until the potatoes are tender.

2 While the potatoes are cooking, warm up the evaporated milk in a separate pot. Add salt and pepper to taste. Add the heated evaporated milk to the potatoes. Add another blob of butter.

3 Drain the juice from the can of clams and add the clams to the chowder. Gently cook the chowder until the clams are heated through, but do not let it boil or the clams will get rubbery.

4 Serve immediately with crackers or fresh bread.

YIELD: 6 servings

— *Lydia Adams*

2 blobs of butter

1 large onion, chopped

6 medium potatoes, cut into small cubes (I leave the jackets on)

1 (14-ounce/385 mL) can evaporated milk

Salt and pepper to taste

1 (142 g) can clams

MINNESOTA PUBLIC RADIO, STORMI GREER

Lydia's Zippy Guacamole Dip

I developed this quick and easy dip for the Maple Leafs' post-season run in 2003. I have found that the hotter I make this dip, the further the Leafs go into the playoffs. You might want to double the recipe to save having to get up and possibly miss a face-off!

One great result of eating this dip is that you will not have a cold for the rest of the season. However, I have to add a warning for choristers: DO NOT UNDER ANY CIRCUMSTANCES ATTEND A CHOIR REHEARSAL UP TO 24 HOURS AFTER EATING THIS DIP. You will NOT be Mr. or Ms. Popularity if you do.

1 Cut open the avocado, remove the pit and spoon the flesh into a dish. (Compost the skins and plant the seed.) Mash with a fork. Add a few sprinkles of sea salt and lots of black pepper. Add the lemon juice to the mashed avocado. (Compost lemon skins and seeds.) Mash the garlic and add it to the mixture. Stir to blend all the ingredients together.

2 If you wish a little more zip, add a few drops of Tabasco sauce.

3 Serve with your favourite chips and beverages.

YIELD: 8 servings

— *Lydia Adams*

1 large ripe avocado

Sea salt and freshly ground black pepper to taste

Juice of ½ juicy lemon

1 large clove garlic (bare minimum—I use at least two per avocado)

Soft Dinner Rolls

MARGIE BOYD
Executive Director

Born in Waterloo, Margie Boyd is a graduate of Waterloo Lutheran University with a degree in psychology. Music has always been an important part of her life, and she is happy to be able to work in the arts without having to perform! In 1986, shortly after moving to Parry Sound, Margie joined the Board of the Festival of the Sound, began to work in the Festival Office in 1989 and took over its management in 1992. She and her husband, Bill, have three adult daughters and take endless delight in their six grandchildren.

Also fondly known as Aunt Margie's Buns, this recipe comes from Camp Tapawingo, on Candle Lake in northern Saskatchewan. Tapawingo, we are told, means a "place of happiness." It was one of our favourite places when our family was young, where we enjoyed good friends, good food, music, laughter, and the wonders of all four seasons. I am always asked to bring these buns to gatherings of our large extended family. I baked nine dozen for one Thanksgiving weekend and had only one bun left on Tuesday morning. The recipe makes a large batch, so there are always lots to share.

1 In a small bowl, stir together the water, yeast, and sugar. Let the mixture proof for 10 minutes, until it is bubbly.

2 In a very large bowl, stir together 10 cups of the flour, the sugar, and salt. Add the warm water, oil, and yeast mixture. Stir with a spoon or with a hand mixer with dough hooks.

3 Gradually add the remaining flour until the mixture is no longer sticky. (You may not need all the flour.) After about 7 cups have been added, turn the dough out of the bowl onto a floured surface. Knead in the last 2 to 3 cups by hand. This takes about 10 minutes. The job is done when the dough is smooth and shiny and no longer sticks to your hands.

4 Place the dough in a well-oiled bowl large enough to contain the dough when it has risen to twice its original size. Turn the dough in the bowl to oil the

1 cup warm water

2 tablespoons active dry yeast

2 teaspoons sugar

20 cups all-purpose flour (approximate)

1 cup sugar

2 teaspoons salt

6 cups warm water

7/8 cup canola oil

(continued on next page)

SARAH BOYD

entire surface, which will prevent the dough from drying out. Let it rise in a warm place until doubled in size, approximately 1½ hours.

5 Punch the dough down in the bowl and again let it rise in a warm place until doubled, approximately 1 hour.

6 Break off pieces of dough about the size of golf balls and shape them into rolls by rolling them on the counter under your loosely cupped hand. Put them on oiled baking pans, cover with a tea towel, and let them rise in a warm place until doubled, approximately ½ hour.

7 Meanwhile, preheat the oven to 400°F. Bake each pan for 15 minutes, until the rolls are golden brown. Cool rolls on racks.

YIELD: 5 dozen rolls

— *Margie Boyd*

"Fried" Chicken

CAROL CAMPBELL
Artistic Director's Advisor

Born in England, Carol met Jim
Campbell in Paris in 1972. In 1976
she came to Canada, supposedly
for six months, and stayed.
Marrying Jim in 1977 probably
had something to do with that.
Celia was born in July 1983,
causing Jim to miss a Festival
concert She advised him against
becoming Artistic Director of the
Festival of the Sound in 1985, as
Graham had just been born and
she felt they were busy enough—
and Jim has not followed her
advice since. The Festival has been
a major part of Carol's life
for more than 20 years, and she
looks forward to returning to
Parry Sound, the family cottage,
the Festival, and their friends
every year.

*I picked this recipe up from a cooking show when I was doing exercises
in front of the TV. I didn't have pen and paper to hand, so the recipe
that I came up with is what I could remember at the end of my exercises.
It's always a big hit with Jim and the family.*

1   In a measuring cup, combine the buttermilk, dry
    mustard, garlic, and salt. Put the chicken pieces in
    a large resealable plastic bag. Pour the buttermilk
    marinade over the chicken, seal, and refrigerate for
    at least 24 hours.

2   Preheat the oven to 400°F.

3   Combine the flour, bread crumbs, cayenne and
    paprika in another plastic bag. Remove the chicken
    from the marinade, discarding the marinade, and
    add one or two pieces at a time to the bread crumb
    mixture, tossing to coat. Arrange the chicken pieces
    skin side up on an oiled baking sheet and spray
    lightly with cooking spray.

4   Bake the chicken for 20 minutes. Turn the pieces
    over and bake them for another 20 minutes, or until
    chicken is cooked through and coating is crisp.

YIELD: 4 to 6 servings

— *Carol Campbell*

1 cup low-fat buttermilk

½ teaspoon dry mustard

2 cloves garlic, minced

Salt to taste

1 chicken, cut into 8 pieces,
or chicken pieces

½ cup all-purpose flour

½ cup dry bread crumbs

A pinch each of cayenne
and paprika

BRUNO SCHRECKER

Granola

I got this recipe from Joanne and David Brunton, who used to run a bed and breakfast in Parry Sound. I choose to use the rye flakes and maple syrup.

1 Preheat the oven to 300°F.

2 In a 13 by 11 by 2-inch baking pan, mix together all of the dry ingredients, except the raisins.

3 In a small saucepan, heat the oil and maple syrup. Pour the heated oil and maple syrup over the dry mix and stir. It helps to dig in with your bare hands to get a good mix.

4 Spread mixture evenly in the roasting pan and bake for 30 minutes, stirring occasionally. For a crunchier granola, bake it a little longer. When cool, stir in the raisins. Store the granola in an airtight container.

YIELD: 10 cups

— *Carol Campbell*

3 cups large-flake rolled oats

1½ cups skim milk powder

1 cup wheat germ

1 cup slivered almonds

1 cup sunflower seeds

½ cup one of the following: rye flakes, oat bran, wheat flakes, or wheat bran

½ cup sesame seeds

¼ cup flax seeds

½ cup canola oil

½ cup maple syrup or honey

1 cup raisins

Lentil and Carrot Salad

I like to keep this summer salad on hand at the cottage. It keeps well in the refrigerator and is nice as part of a buffet (simply triple the recipe).

1 Combine the lentils, carrots, garlic, bay leaf, thyme, and salt in a saucepan. Add enough stock to cover the lentils by at least 1 inch. Bring to a boil, reduce the heat and simmer, uncovered, for 15 minutes, or until the lentils are just tender. Add the onion and celery in the last few minutes of cooking.

2 Drain the lentil mixture, reserving 3 tablespoons of the stock. Discard the bay leaf. Transfer the lentil mixture to a serving bowl, stir in the parsley and pepper, and toss with 2 or 3 tablespoons of the reserved stock in place of salad dressing.

YIELD: 4 to 6 servings

— *Carol Campbell*

1 cup brown lentils

1 cup finely diced carrots

2 garlic cloves, minced

1 bay leaf

½ teaspoon thyme

Salt to taste

2 cups chicken stock

1 cup finely diced onion

½ cup finely diced celery

¼ cup chopped fresh parsley

Pepper to taste

Marinated Veggies

JAMES CAMPBELL
Artistic Director

James Campbell, Artistic Director of the Festival of the Sound, has been called "Canada's pre-eminent clarinetist and wind soloist" by the *Toronto Star*. Following his June 2004 performance with the Boston Pops, the *Boston Globe* wrote, "James Campbell made a sensationally virtuosic and versatile soloist." He has collaborated with many of the world's great musicians, including five television programs with the late Glenn Gould. In 1997, James Campbell was made a member of the Order of Canada. He is a professor of music at Indiana University, residing there during the academic year and returning to his lakeside home near Parry Sound each summer.

This recipe is from my mother, Marjorie Campbell. This salad is a tasty addition to a buffet. You may choose other vegetables, according to your preference.

1 Working with one vegetable at a time, blanch the cauliflower and carrots in boiling water until they are partially cooked but not soft. Drain and cover with cold water to prevent further cooking, and drain again.

2 In a large bowl, stir together the soup, sugar, oil, vinegar, mustard, Worcestershire sauce, and salt and pepper. Add the blanched vegetables, green peppers, and onion. Marinate overnight, covered and refrigerated. Stir just before serving.

YIELD: 8 to 12 servings as a buffet dish or antipasto

— *Jim Campbell*

1 cauliflower, broken into bite-sized pieces

2 cups carrots cut into medallions (about 5 medium carrots)

1 (10-ounce/284 mL) can tomato soup

¾ cup sugar

½ cup vegetable oil

½ cup white vinegar

1 teaspoon prepared mustard

1 teaspoon Worcestershire sauce

Salt and pepper to taste

2 green peppers, cut into bite-sized pieces

1 onion, coarsely chopped

BRUNO SCHRECKER

Marmalade

Jim's wife, Carol, makes this marmalade for him regularly because it tastes so much better than the store-bought varieties. If you have no lemons, add extra oranges.

1   Wash the fruit and slice very thinly, discarding the seeds and end pieces. Cut the oranges and lemons into quarters; cut the grapefruits into eighths.

2   Put the fruit and water into a large saucepan. Bring the water to a boil. Add the sugar and return to a boil.

3   Reduce the heat, cover, and simmer, stirring occasionally, until the mixture thickens, 2 to 3 hours, skimming any foam from the surface if necessary. Uncover and simmer for 15 minutes. Place a small plate in the freezer.

4   Test for gel point: Remove the pot from the heat. Spoon a little marmalade onto the cold plate and return it to the freezer for a few minutes. The marmalade is ready when it does not run together when separated with a spoon. If it is not thick enough, continue to simmer the marmalade, testing every couple of minutes.

5   Bottle in sterilized jars.

YIELD: 6 to 7 (16-ounce) jars

— *Jim Campbell*

6 medium oranges
(any kind you like)

2 grapefruits
(any kind you like)

2 lemons

2 cups water

9 cups sugar

Mincemeat

This delicious recipe makes wonderful mince pies and tarts at Christmas!

1 Peel and finely dice the apple. In a large bowl, toss it with a little lemon juice to prevent it from discolouring. Set aside.

2 Put the raisins and currants through a grinder, very slowly so the grinder won't clog up. Add the raisins and currants to the apple along with the sugar, brandy, margarine, mixed spice, ginger, nutmeg, cinnamon, and orange zest. Combine well.

3 Cover the mixture and let it sit at room temperature for 24 hours.

4 Spoon the mincemeat into sterilized jars, and store it for at least 2 weeks before using.

YIELD: 2 pints

HINTS: These ingredients aren't written in stone. You can add or leave out anything to your own taste.

Do not double the ingredients, hoping to make a larger batch, because the mixing becomes very difficult. Take the time to mix well.

— *Jim Campbell*

1 apple

1 cup dark raisins

½ cup golden raisins

1 cup currants

1 cup brown sugar

3 tablespoons brandy

2 tablespoons margarine, melted

½ teaspoon mixed spice*

¼ teaspoon ground ginger

¼ teaspoon nutmeg

¼ teaspoon cinnamon

Zest of 1 orange or grapefruit

*You can make your own English mixed spice by stirring together equal amounts of ground cloves, mace, grated nutmeg, ground coriander, and allspice with a pinch of cinnamon.

Pear and Parsnip Soup

This wonderful soup recipe comes from our dear friend Joan Reed-Olsen, who is a long-time worker and supporter of the Festival. Joan's gracious home in the Beach neighbourhood of Toronto has provided a refreshing home away from home to many musicians in their travels to and from Parry Sound.

1 Heat the oil in a large saucepan over medium heat. Cook the leeks, stirring frequently, until soft. Add the parsnips and carrots, and cook, stirring occasionally, until soft, about 10 minutes.

2 Stir in the pears, sage, thyme, cinnamon, and nutmeg. Add the wine and simmer for 7 to 10 minutes.

3 Add the water. Simmer for another 10 to 15 minutes. Season with salt and pepper.

4 Purée the soup in a blender, working in batches if necessary. Return soup to the pot and stir in the cream (if using). Reheat the soup, but do not allow it to boil.

5 Serve garnished with the Gouda and pear slices.

YIELD: 4 to 6 servings

— *Jim Campbell*

¼ cup olive oil

1 cup thinly sliced leeks (white part only)

3 cups diced parsnips

1 cup diced carrots

3 cups diced peeled pears (about 3 pears)

2 tablespoons chopped fresh sage

2 tablespoons chopped fresh thyme

1 teaspoon cinnamon

½ teaspoon nutmeg

½ cup white wine

4 cups water

Salt and pepper to taste

½ cup light cream (optional)

Shredded smoked Gouda and slices of pear, for garnish

Pecan Balls

RONA HOKANSON
Lecturer

Rona Hokanson was executive director of the U.S.A. International Harp competition held in Bloomington, Indiana, until her retirement. Previously, she was assistant to the director of the International Music Competition of the German broadcasting network, held each year in Munich. Rona's husband, pianist Leonard Hokanson, was internationally recognized as a recitalist, soloist, and chamber musician. One of the last pupils of Artur Schnabel, he was a professor of piano at the renowned School of Music at Indiana University.

1 Preheat the oven to 350°F. Grease a cookie sheet.

2 Cream together the butter and sugar. Stir in the flour, pecans, and vanilla.

3 Roll the batter into small balls, each about 1 inch in diameter. Arrange balls on the cookie sheet. Bake 20 minutes. Allow the balls to cool for 5 minutes.

4 Roll the pecan balls gently in the confectioners' sugar. Store the balls in an airtight container.

YIELD: approximately 30 pecan balls

— *Rona Hokanson*

¼ pound butter (½ cup)

2 tablespoons sugar

1 cup all-purpose flour

4 ounces (100 grams) ground pecans

1 teaspoon vanilla

Confectioners' sugar

Walnut Snails

ANTON KUERTI KRISTINE BOGYO
Founding Artistic Directors

At the age of 11, pianist Anton Kuerti performed the Grieg Concerto with Arthur Fiedler and, while still a student, won the Leventritt Award. Anton's vast repertoire features some 50 concertos, including one he composed himself. He was, for many years, a professor at the University of Toronto but now devotes himself entirely to performing, composing, and giving master classes. Anton is the founding Artistic Director of the Festival of the Sound. His wife, cellist Kristine Bogyo, is also a Festival regular. Kristine is the founder and Music Director of Mooredale Concerts and conductor of the Mooredale Youth Orchestra.

This is Kristine's grandmother's recipe. Everyone in the Kuerti family loves it.

1 Preheat the oven to 350°F.

2 In a large bowl, combine the flour, butter, 2 tablespoons of the sugar, the egg yolks, yeast, and salt. Knead with your hands until a dough forms. Add a bit of milk, if necessary, to make a pliable dough. Divide the dough in half, and roll out each piece into a thin oval, about ⅛ inch thick.

3 In a small bowl mix together the ground walnuts and the remaining ¾ cup sugar. In a separate bowl, beat the egg whites until they stand in stiff peaks. Fold the egg whites into the nut mixture. Spread the filling evenly over each round of dough.

4 Roll up each disc from the long side to make two loaves, and cut them into slices about a finger thick. Place the slices on a cookie sheet about 1 inch apart.

5 Bake for half an hour, or until golden brown. Cool on a rack.

YIELD: about 24 cookies

— *Anton Kuerti and Kristine Bogyo*

4 cups all-purpose flour

½ pound unsalted butter (1 cup), softened

¾ cup plus 2 tablespoons sugar

4 egg yolks

1 package quick-rise yeast

A pinch of salt

Milk, if necessary

200 grams finely ground walnuts*

4 egg whites

*Do not grind the nuts in a blender or food processor. They will become too sticky. Buy ground walnuts at a bulk-food store or in packages at a grocery store. They should be dry like flour.

MORLEY MARKSON

Pasta with Shrimp in Tomato Cream

GARY KULESHA
Composer

Gary Kulesha was born in Toronto in 1954. Although principally a composer, he is active as both a pianist and a conductor and has appeared and recorded in both roles in premieres of new works by several composers as well as in standard repertoire. Gary's compositions have been commissioned and performed by noted artists all over the world. Gary Kulesha is Composer-Advisor to the Toronto Symphony Orchestra. He resides in Toronto with his wife, composer Larysa Kuzmenko.

Sun-dried tomatoes join shrimp, basil, and cream to make an elegant sauce for linguine.

1 Measure 2 tablespoons of the oil from the tomatoes. Set the tomatoes aside.

2 Heat the oil in a large skillet over medium-high heat. When the oil is hot, add the garlic and shrimp. Cook, stirring often, until the shrimp are opaque in the centre, about 2½ minutes. Lift out shrimp and set aside.

3 Add the onions, chopped basil, pepper, vermouth, broth, and cream to the pan. Boil over high heat, stirring occasionally, until reduced to about 1½ cups, about 10 minutes. Add the sun-dried tomatoes and the shrimp to the sauce. Stir until just heated through.

4 Meanwhile, in a large pot of boiling salted water, cook the linguine until al dente. Drain the linguine and arrange it on dinner plates.

5 Spoon the sauce over the pasta. Garnish with basil, if desired. Serve with Parmesan cheese.

YIELD: 4 servings

— Gary Kulesha

⅓ cup sun-dried tomatoes packed in oil, drained (reserve the oil) and slivered

1 clove garlic, minced or pressed

1 pound large shrimp, peeled and deveined

¼ cup thinly sliced green onions, including tops

1½ tablespoons chopped fresh basil (or 1 teaspoon dried)

¼ teaspoon white pepper

¾ cup dry vermouth

1 cup chicken broth

1 cup heavy cream

10 ounces linguine

Fresh basil sprigs, if desired

Grated Parmesan cheese

Brandied Chicken Breasts

LARYSA KUZMENKO
Composer

Larysa Kuzmenko is a Toronto-based composer and pianist. Her music has been performed and broadcast throughout the world. Larysa studied with Oskar Morawetz and Walter Buczynski at the University of Toronto, where she received her master's degree in composition. She has had a number of works commissioned by the Ontario Arts Council and has had her compositions performed numerous times. Ms. Kuzmenko is currently on the staffs of the Royal Conservatory of Music and the Faculty of Music at the University of Toronto, where she teaches piano, theory, harmony, and history.

If you're not strong enough of heart to go to the barn and slaughter a couple of young chickens, you may use 4 skinless, boneless chicken breasts from your local butcher.

1 Rub the chicken breasts with brandy. Let stand for about 10 minutes, and then season them with salt, pepper, and marjoram.

2 Melt the butter in a skillet over medium heat to the point of fragrance. Sauté the chicken for 6 to 8 minutes on each side. Transfer them to a heated ovenproof platter, and keep warm.

3 Add the sherry to the pan. Simmer over low heat until the liquid is reduced to half, about 15 minutes. Meanwhile, preheat the broiler.

4 In a medium bowl, beat together the cream, egg yolks, salt, pepper, and nutmeg. Add the egg mixture to the pan, stirring constantly. Cook, stirring, until slightly thickened.

5 Pour the sauce over the chicken breasts. Sprinkle with the cheese–bread crumb mixture. Broil until glazed.

YIELD: 4 servings

— *Larysa Kuzmenko*

Skinless, boneless breasts from 2 young chickens

Brandy

Salt, pepper, and dried marjoram to taste

6 tablespoons unsalted butter

½ cup dry sherry

2 cups heavy cream

4 egg yolks

Salt, pepper, and nutmeg to taste

¼ cup shredded Swiss cheese

¼ cup dry bread crumbs tossed with 1 tablespoon melted butter

Easy Sautéed Shrimp

CHARLES W. STOCKEY
Benefactor

Charles Stockey was born in 1917 in Toronto and spent his boyhood exploring the fields, ravines, and rivers near his home. As a young person, he was introduced to the Parry Sound area and developed a life-long love for music and fine art. Those two loves came together when he built a home on Lake Joseph and became a volunteer for the Festival of the Sound. In 1988, Charles and his wife, Lois, moved to Victoria, B.C. In the last two and a half years of his life, with the naming of the Charles W. Stockey Centre for the Performing Arts, Charles found a special joy and a new circle of friends and left his mark on the world in a wonderful way.

This is a recipe that I picked up in that country of wonderful food—South Louisiana. It's easy—it's delightful—a favourite! Do not overcook the shrimp! It only toughens them. I serve the shrimp in the sauce, and we like to dip French bread into it as we eat the shrimp. The shrimp are also good the next day in a green salad. Bon appétit!

1 Heat a large skillet over medium heat. Pour in the salad dressing, and gently simmer it, stirring occasionally, until you can no longer smell the vinegar. This should take about 15 minutes.

2 Add the butter and the beer. Stir everything together. When the butter melts, reduce the heat to low and continue cooking until you can no longer smell the beer. Season the sauce with salt, pepper and Tabasco sauce (if using).

3 Drop the shrimp into the pan and gently cook them on low heat until they turn pink, 2 to 3 minutes. Remove the shrimp from the sauce, and transfer them to a serving dish.

HINT: You can do one or two things with the leftover sautéing liquid, if you don't serve it with the shrimp. Save it in a container in the refrigerator so it's ready the next time you need it, or put it back on the stove, set the heat to medium-low, and stir in a couple of teaspoons of arrowroot or cornstarch. This will give you a sauce that can be served over rice or potatoes.

YIELD: 2 servings

— *Charles W. Stockey*

1 (16-ounce/475 mL) bottle Kraft Zesty Italian Salad Dressing

½ cup unsalted butter

½ cup beer

Salt and pepper to taste

Tabasco sauce to taste (optional)

1 pound shrimp, peeled (I like the large ones)

Index